Praise

In a climate change debate pumped full of duplicity and evasion, Javier Sethness-Castro blasts in air-clearing testament to the calamity facing humanity. Sethness-Castro argues boldly that humanity is the asteroid this time, responsible for one of the great extinctions in earth's history. *Imperiled Life* is no halfhearted call to shuffle the lightbulbs on a sinking terrestrial *Titanic*. It demands we rethink our philosophies, reorganize our societies, and rework our economies if we are to escape a fate of being survived only by valleys of bones and mountains of garbage.

—Arun Gupta, cofounder of the *Indypendent* and the *Occupied Wall Street Journal*

Javier Sethness-Castro here importantly diagnoses the ways in which today's dominant trends toward fascist authoritarianism, casino capitalism, and cataclysmic militarism ominously intend a planetary future predicated on widespread genocide, ecological collapse, and the enclosure of moral progress. Moreover, *Imperiled Life* provides hope that social movements around the world are actively struggling to find common insurgent cause together—to democratically occupy the global power structure, work for human, animal, and earth liberation, and create sustainable community alternatives. May this fundamentally change the political climate of our future such that justice, peace, and happiness on Earth are more than just utopian urges or filthy privileges of the super affluent!

—Richard Kahn, author of *Critical Pedagogy, Ecoliteracy, and Planetary Crisis*

This is an extremely well-researched and well-written book, providing both a history of our awareness of the coming global environmental collapse, and a plausible and even inspiring plan for present and future action. The more people who read it, the better humanity's chances will be.

—Kim Stanley Robinson, author of *Green Mars*

Imperiled Life is an angry and urgent dissection of the omnivorous economic system that is mercilessly turning the planet into a death camp.

—Jeffrey St. Clair, coeditor of *Counterpunch* and author of *Born Under a Bad Sky*

IMPERILED LIFE

REVOLUTION AGAINST CLIMATE CATASTROPHE

Imperiled Life: Revolution against Climate Catastrophe
by Javier Sethness-Castro

ISBN 978 1 849351 05 8 | Ebook: 978 1 849351 06 5
Library of Congress Number: 2012937633

© 2012 Javier Sethness-Castro

This edition © 2012 AK Press and the Institute for Anarchist Studies
Cover Design and Interior: Josh MacPhee/Justseeds.org

Illustrations: Santiago Armengod/Justseeds.org
Printed the USA on recycled, acid-free paper by union labor

AK Press, 674-A 23rd Street, Oakland, CA 94612
www.akpress.org, | akpress@akpress.org | 510.208.1700

AK Press U.K., PO Box 12766, Edinburgh EH8 9YE
www.akuk.com | ak@akedin.demon.co.uk | 0131.555.5165

Institute for Anarchist Studies, P.O. Box 15586, Washington, DC 20003
www.anarchist-studies.org | info@anarchiststudies.org

At least 50 percent of the net sales from each title in the Anarchist
Interventions series are donated to the IAS, thanks to the generosity
of each author.

IMPERILED LIFE

REVOLUTION AGAINST CLIMATE CATASTROPHE

Javier Sethness-Castro

AK Press / Institute for Anarchist Studies | 2012

Anarchist Interventions:
An IAS/AK Press Book Series

Radical ideas can open up spaces for radical actions, by illuminating hierarchical power relations and drawing out possibilities for liberatory social transformations. The Anarchist Interventions series—a collaborative project between the Institute for Anarchist Studies (IAS) and AK Press—strives to contribute to the development of relevant, vital anarchist theory and analysis by intervening in contemporary discussions. Works in this series will look at twenty-first-century social conditions—including social structures and oppression, their historical trajectories, and new forms of domination, to name a few—as well as reveal opportunities for different tomorrows premised on horizontal, egalitarian forms of self-organization.

Given that anarchism has become the dominant tendency within revolutionary milieus and movements today, it is crucial that anarchists explore current phenomena, strategies, and visions in a much more rigorous, serious manner. Each title in this series, then, will feature a present-day anarchist voice, with the aim, over time, of publishing a variety of perspectives. The series' multifaceted goals are to cultivate anarchist thought so as to better inform anarchist practice, encourage a culture of public intellectuals and constructive debate within anarchism, introduce new generations to anarchism, and offer insights into today's world and potentialities for a freer society.

Contents

Foreword by Paul Messersmith-Glavin 1
Acknowledgments 10
Prologue: Cancún and Catastrophe 13

1 The Death of Life? 33
2 Fragmentary Critique 57
3 On Hope and Reason Today 73
4 On Adorno's New Categorical Imperative 111
5 For an Ecological Anarcho-Communism 137

Notes 179
Credits for Anarchist Interventions 217

Foreword

The basic structure of capitalism is at the heart of the climate crisis. Carbon emissions, the primary source of our changing climate, are the by-product of industrial production. Capitalism is literally changing the weather. Often, industry is blamed for climate change. People frequently talk about burning oil and coal, or fault cars and factories, but this misses the underlying dynamic that ties all these things together: industry is an expression of a system. Ascending over the last four hundred years, capitalism continues to be the dominant organizing force in the world, shaping life as we know it. All attempts at slowing—much less stopping—its growth have failed. The emission of climate-changing gases is intrinsic to the capitalist logic. Every day that this continues, the climate will continue to change. The year 2010 saw the highest emission of greenhouse gases in history.

Capitalism is based on a philosophy of "grow or die" and ruthless competition; companies need to continually expand and grow, or they will not survive. It is a system that seeks to maximize profit by exploiting labor as well as treating nature as both a "resource" and garbage dump. Despite all the warning signs—such as news of drought, heat waves, and new species being threatened by changing habitat—and what scientists say, the system marches on, with absolutely no sign of letting up. That is because it cannot change its fundamental nature. It is a form of economic and social organization at odds with nature and human community that has come to shape nearly everything in life, such that we can hardly imagine the possibility of life outside capitalism. It promotes qualities like greed and selfishness, and creates us in its image. Capitalism is more than an economic system; it is a way of life. Maximizing profit at the expense of all else is its very metabolism. To stop catastrophic climate change, we must stop capitalism.

So what is capitalism? At its core, it is based on only paying a worker the worth of a portion of their work. The owner keeps the remaining worth, or value. This "surplus value" is one of the sources of profit. Thus capitalism is an organized system of theft, wherein those who actually do the work are not paid the full value of their effort. The owners keep as profit the difference between the value that is created by the worker and that which the worker is paid as a wage. Because it is a system designed by and for capitalists, workers are necessarily exploited and mistreated. It is this same focus on profit that sees nature as a place where materials are found and then converted into commodities, with an emphasis on doing this as cheaply as possible. The way in which materials are obtained from nature is guided not by any thought about the integrity of nature itself, or the delicate balance of natural processes. It is guided by making money, pure and simple. The same is true at the other end of the productive process, when toxic chemicals and by-products are dumped as cheaply as possible. Hence owners fight attempts to regulate their ability to pollute. Not polluting costs money. It costs money to buy filters and scrubbers to limit toxic emissions, or to research and develop alternative sources of energy, and all this cuts into profits. Generally the fines for polluting are so insignificant that owners calculate that it is more worthwhile to pollute and pay the fines rather than, for example, upgrading their machinery to satisfy clean air or water regulations. This is a system ruled by the bottom line.

To stop capitalism, we need a social and political movement. This past year, 2011, marked the emergence of just such a movement. The Arab Spring saw millions of people rise up in opposition to long-standing tyrannical regimes. Some of these governments fell. Millions of people occupied prominent squares and did not back down against the power of states. This inspired people in the United States to launch their own movement—an occupation movement at Wall Street, the symbolic heart of global capitalism. Occupy Wall Street (OWS), which spread around the United States, Canada, and the world, is a populist movement that challenges the economic control of what they call the 1 percent. OWS champions the 99 percent, or those without great sources of wealth. This is significant because it points to the machinations of the 1 percent, or ruling class, and suggests the possibility of creating what Antonio Gramsci calls a "counterhegemonic" movement. For Gramsci, ruling-class ideas are the dominant ones. They are so widely propagated that they become "common sense." An example is the belief that the sign of a healthy economy is vigorous growth. Or that to be a productive member of society, you have to have a job, which basically discounts stay-at-home parents, many artists, self-sufficient farmers, and others, while valuing only those who are enmeshed in the dominant economy. It is this common sense that serves the interests of the capitalist class. The OWS protests represent the development of an ideological alternative that puts the interests of everyday, working people ahead of those of the rulers. OWS has successfully changed the nature of discussion in the United States, forcing issues of economic equality and social justice onto the agenda. It signals a good beginning.

In addition to challenging ruling-class economic ideas, or those held by the 1 percent, OWS has put ideals of direct democracy, long championed by anarchists and other antiauthoritarians, into practice. The use of general assemblies as policymaking bodies and the reliance on modified forms of consensus decision making, however problematic consensus may be in certain situations, both have long histories within antiauthoritarian leftist movements. This new movement hopes to unite the majority against the minority currently running the show.

The historic development of capitalism is intertwined with colonialism, and later, neocolonialism. The economy, in its never-ending need to expand and accumulate, resolved early crises by going to the so-called third world to seek resources for production and sources of cheap—or in the case of slavery, free—labor. By waging war and asserting its military dominance, Europe was able to control vast territory from which raw materials could be obtained. European colonialism, the North American slave trade, and later neocolonial domination such as the Algerian and Vietnam wars all represent the attempted dominance of what was once called the first world over the peoples of the so-called third world. This is a racist dynamic in which the largely white, European people of the North dominate and exploit the people of the South. And it is exactly these people, the poor of the Southern Hemisphere, who will suffer the most from the changing climate. They already are suffering, as attested to by the recent floods that devastated Pakistan and Thailand along with the droughts that ravaged Mexico and Africa.

It will take a sustained movement to fundamentally transform society and stop climate change. Such revolutionary change will require a democratically controlled economy that puts human needs and ecological integrity ahead of short-term profit. It will require instituting directly democratic ways of making political decisions, so that the people affected by the outcomes are the ones with the power to determine solutions.

OWS began at Zuccotti Park, once called Liberty Plaza. It was at this same Liberty Plaza twenty years earlier that an organization called the Youth Greens met in the chilly, predawn hours the day after the twentieth Earth Day anniversary to challenge what it saw as the primary cause of the ecological crisis: capitalism, as symbolized by the institution of Wall Street. In solidarity with the Wall Street

Action—which was endorsed by over fifty social and political groups, and turned out two thousand people organized into affinity groups, with close to three hundred arrested—actions were held in San Francisco, Eugene (Oregon), Minneapolis, and St. Louis. In San Francisco, six hundred people marched on the Pacific Stock Exchange at 6:00 a.m., with fifty of those later arrested.

The Youth Greens was largely an ecological anarchist organization, working with the Green movement of the 1980s and 1990s. It had active chapters in five U.S. cities, with annual decision-making conferences, and infused antiauthoritarian ideas and practices into the emerging Green movement, arguing against reformists. The Youth Greens asserted that the ecological crisis was a result of social forms of domination, and that humans dominating and exploiting other humans extended into the natural world in the attempt to dominate nature. Thus, for the Youth Greens and its allies in the Left Green Network, resolving the social crisis, by addressing and overturning all forms of social hierarchy and domination, was the only way to solve the ecological crisis.

We can learn from the ideas and practices of the Youth Greens. At the Earth Day Wall Street Action, Youth Greens assembled the first black bloc in the United States—inspired by the German *autonomen*, or "those who are autonomous." Dozens of young people dressed in all black and covered their faces with black bandanas as a way to avoid being identified and surveilled by police. Nine years later, this tactic would gain worldwide visibility at the World Trade Organization protests in Seattle. The Youth Greens also developed political principles covering almost every aspect of contemporary life, from gay and lesbian liberation to anti-racism to the practice of direct democracy, viewing all this as interrelated and part of a larger global movement.

As new movements continue, we need to incorporate an ecological sensibility and understanding of how capitalism—which is responsible for most of the social ills being protested—is also responsible for changing the climate. We will need to fundamentally reorganize society to not only ensure social and economic justice but also preserve humanity. For humanity to thrive, capitalism must die. Climate change is racist. Whether dubbed the 1 percent or the ruling class, the people who control the countries of the Northern Hemisphere are sacrificing the lives of largely poor people of color to maintain their rule and accumulate wealth. The most privileged people on the planet are letting millions of the less fortunate suffer and die. Three hundred thousand people a year are dying, mostly the poor of the Southern Hemisphere, due to the climate catastrophe. This number will only increase every year that things do not change.

Instead of acting to stop the emission of greenhouse gases, the so-called 1 percent is reorienting its military to adapt to changing climate conditions. The military is the part of the U.S. government that actually takes climate change seriously. The Pentagon, taking climate change as a given, is planning on fighting all the wars that will be necessitated by imperialism within the emerging context of drought, famine, mass death, and millions of refugees. Whereas recent U.S. wars have been in part over the control of oil, future wars will be in response to the destabilizing effects of climate change. It is a vicious dialectic in which oil and coal continue to propel the economy, then wars are fought to maintain control over those resources, and further wars are fought to respond to the results of climate change that stem from relying on those forms of energy.

To be most profitable, capitalism seeks the cheapest sources of energy. These happen to be oil and coal. Control of these "resources" is also highly profitable. The entire capitalist apparatus is built on the exploitation of oil and coal. Despite all the warning signs and reports from scientists, the dominant economic system is pushing irrationally to exploit the remaining reserves of oil and coal through the ecologically disastrous tar sands mining operations in Canada, fracking and mountain top removal in Appalachia, and oil drilling in pristine areas of Alaska and along the ocean shores. Capitalism has become an obsessive, hungry ghost, wanting more and more, despite its inevitable doom.

My child will be born this year. If our society does not change fundamentally in his lifetime, the world will be a very different place by the time he reaches old age. In 2112, life on Earth may be unrecognizable. He and his generation will likely ask us what we did to stop this madness when we still had time. Some scientists say we need to reduce carbon output by 90 percent by 2020, and others assert we need to drastically cut emissions by 2015. What is inarguable is that the time to act is now. We know what is happening and what we must do. What stops us? If our children and our children's children are to have a life worth living, we must act.

This book is an impassioned plea for sanity, reason, and justice. It breaks through the collective denial we indulge in to call attention to the perilous nature of life. The weather is changing—that is clear. Crucially, though, the climate is changing. This is the long-term, underlying reality behind the changes in the weather. Severe weather events are becoming common, such as floods, storms, and extremes of hot and cold. We all know something is not right. Matters will only get worse unless we act. But to act, we need to know what to do. We need to understand what is happening. *Imperiled Life* is a critical reflection on what is going on, and why. It contains diagnosis, prognosis, and remedies. The diagnosis is clear, the prognosis is not good, and the remedies are extreme and radical. These are the times in which we live.

Javier Sethness-Castro, like the critical theorists of the Frankfurt school in whose tradition he writes, invites the reader to come and think with him. This book is an invitation to an honest reflection on our changing climate. It is thoughtful, angry, pessimistic, but ultimately hopeful. It asks us to be bold, remake the world, overthrow capitalism, and create a directly democratic, ecological society, in which we live in harmony with nature and each other. We need a society that does not change the weather or exploit humans, and one that leaves the world a better place for future generations. Enjoy reading and, as importantly, act to change the world.

—Paul Messersmith-Glavin

Acknowledgments

I would like to thank my primary editor Paul Messersmith-Glavin for his solidarity, patience, and kindness over the course of this work. I also am indebted to Cindy Milstein for the copyediting, Josh MacPhee for his book design, Zach Blue for the layout and proofreading, and Santiago Armengod for sharing his wondrous art. Moreover, I would like to recognize and thank everyone with the Institute for Anarchist Studies and AK Press for agreeing to include *Imperiled Life* in the Anarchist Interventions series in the first place.

In addition, I am grateful to my mother and father for their support over the years. I would also like to acknowledge my past formal instructors Peter Wright, Michael Mason, David Goldfrank, Robert Bruce Douglass, and Raymundo Sánchez for their enlightenment and aid, along with Binu Mathew and Ian Angus, who kindly served as editors for some of the writings that predate and foreshadow this work. Beyond these individuals, I would like particularly to thank Clark Donley, Brian Lynch, and Daniela McBane, who served as informal editors and advisers on the developing manuscript. I greatly appreciate all those who agreed to provide review blurbs for the book as well. Lastly, I would like to thank the following comrades and colleagues for their love and friendship: Liz López, Jakob Rieken, Aris Chatzinikoloau, Costas Stratilatis, Nancy Moreno, Allen Kim, Marcus Benigno, Sierra Lapoint, Andrew Stefan, Philippe Goute, Cristian Guerrero, Max Hoiland, Jonathan Carl Vogel, Andrew Enciso, Nate Pitts, and Alexei Hong.

As regards this work's title, I am indebted to feminist queer theorist Judith Butler's 2004 work *Precarious Life*, and the call posited by antinuclear thinker and activist Günther Anders in his 1955 work *Hiroshima ist Überall* (Hiroshima Is Everywhere): "Imperiled of all lands, unite!"

I dedicate this work to Bety Cariño, Jyri Jaakkola, the children of Nablus, Betsy Boyd, Vittorio Arrigoni, Javier Torres Cruz, and many others.

—Javier Sethness-Castro

Prologue: Cancún and Catastrophe

> We turn a blind eye to what surrounds us and a deaf ear
> to humanity's never-ending cry.
> —Alain Resnais, *Nuit et Broillard*

The survival of humanity is imperiled. Whereas the prospect of humanity's collective suicide through nuclear war seemed a plausible threat during much of the twentieth century, today the specter of catastrophic climate change has eclipsed nuclear annihilation in this horrifying role. The dangerous human interference with Earth's climate systems that has been driven by the historical rise of capitalism stands within the near future to destroy the very material conditions on which much of life—humanity as well as other beings—depends for its reproduction and sustenance. Basic reflection bears this out.

Average global temperatures in 2010 were tied with those of 2005, when Earth experienced the hottest temperatures observed since people started keeping records in 1880.[1] The average global temperature of the planet has risen 0.8°C (1.4°F) since the beginning of industrialization. Atmospheric concentrations of carbon dioxide have risen from an estimated preindustrial level of 280 parts per million (ppm) to 394 ppm—the level found in May 2011.[2] The rate of annual percentage increase in carbon emissions has in fact accelerated in recent years, exceeding the worst-case scenarios considered by the Intergovernmental Panel on Climate Change (IPCC) in its 2007 *Fourth Annual Report*, the most recent of its periodic assessments of the state of the planet's climate.[3] Carbon emissions in 2010 were the highest ever recorded, despite the ongoing recession.[4] As the International Energy Agency notes, the continued reproduction of such trends in the foreseeable future would entirely jeopardize hopes for limiting climate change to a 2°C (3.6°F) rise in average global temperatures, the warming threshold considered "safe." Worse, a climatological study released just before the 2010 Copenhagen climate negotiations found the world to be on course for a 6°C (10.5°F) rise in average global temperatures by the end of the present century.[5] Change on such a destructive scale would undoubtedly result in mass death among humans as agriculture generally fails, water supplies significantly diminish, and diseases spread. Billions of people would be expected to die under such conditions, as British Earth scientist James Lovelock has warned.[6] British climatologist Kevin Anderson estimates that a mere 10 percent of the present human population—around a half-billion people—would survive a 4°C–6°C (7°F –10.5°F) increase.[7]

Plainly stated, much of humanity, together with future generations, is being sacrificed in the interest of what Marxist U.S. geographer David Harvey terms "the two primary systemic agents in our time": capital and the state.[8] This consideration is readily observed in the behavior engaged in by the world's states at the November–December 2010 Conference of Parties (COP16) to the United Nations Framework Convention on Climate Change held in Cancún, Mexico, as in other exercises in absurdist theater that pass for climate negotiations. That Cancún's Moon Palace, the forum for the talks, is located less than two hundred miles from the Chicxulub site—the location of the impact crater of the infamous asteroid that, striking Earth 65 million years ago, is believed to have induced the mass-extinction event that destroyed the dinosaurs and approximately half of all other existing species—seems fitting, for a similar mass-extinction event is currently being enacted by global capitalism, with present extinction rates having been estimated in 2004 to be a hundred to a thousand times the "background" or average extinction rate observed in Earth's fossil record.[9] Indeed, of the 8.7 million species estimated in August 2011 to exist on Earth, many are expected to go extinct well before being discovered by science.[10] Whether the present extinction crisis will be as near terminal as that experienced during the Great Dying visited on Earth 251 million years ago in the Permian Age, when over 90 percent of all existing species perished, remains to be seen. It bears noting that the Permian Age, unlike the end-Cretaceous extinction event that began at Chicxulub, is thought to have been caused not by asteroid impact but rather by catastrophic climate change induced by intense volcanic activity that was accelerated through positive-feedback mechanisms that ultimately synergized in dismantling the planet's protective ozone layer. Unless radically interrupted, the life destruction currently being prosecuted by global capitalism will be similarly catastrophic.

Such reflections militate sharply against German idealist George Wilhelm Friedrich Hegel's interpretation of human history—the dubious notion that "the Real is the rational, and the rational is the Real"—as well as other manners of understanding and relating to the world denounced by antiauthoritarian French psychoanalyst Félix Guattari as being "sedative"—that is, ones that render invisible the acute suffering perpetrated by the profoundly wrong nature of existing society.[11] In place of this, reflection on the present climate predicament, taken alongside consideration of the threat of imperial war and other potential relapses, could come close to German Marxists Max Horkheimer and Theodor W. Adorno's assertion in the mid-1940s that the "dialectic of Enlightenment" as well as the chance for human progress generally have failed to bring about an emancipated humanity that does not dominate nature, and have instead ushered in a "world radiant with calamity."[12] Guattari was in this sense far too optimistic in his 1989 warning that "there is at least a risk that there will be no more human history unless humanity undertakes a radical reconsideration of itself."[13] It instead now seems to be the case that the chance for "continued progress" necessitates the "radical subversion of the prevailing direction and organization of progress," as German critical theorist Herbert Marcuse recommends, together with the institution of the categorical imperative identified by Karl Marx in his early reflections on religion: that humanity *"overthrow all relations* in which man [*sic*] is a debased, enslaved, abandoned, contemptible being."[14]

The world has long been calamitous, of course. Before the threat posed by climate change came to be understood, the destructions of Vietnam and Iraq were prosecuted, just decades after the attempted extermination of European Jewry along with the nuclear bombings of Hiroshima and Nagasaki. Before these world-historical regressions occurred were the myriad horrors of the First World War. Preceding this mindless conflict were European colonialism and genocides as practiced against southern peoples. The year 1492 CE, when the European powers began destroying the peoples indigenous to what would later be referred to as North and South America, was the same year in which chauvinist Spaniards defeated the Moors, and expelled large swathes of Jews and Muslims from the lands subsequently claimed by the Catholic monarchy. The Crusades as well as the Roman Empire mimicked the ethnocide and slavery engaged in by centralized power since the historical rise of empires in Mesopotamia and later Egypt. The reign of czars, kings, and emperors mirrors the regression that overthrew original nonhierarchical societies. Hannah Arendt, a compelling twentieth-century critic of authority and totalitarianism, rightly notes that "any long-range view of history"—or at least recorded human history—"is not very encouraging."[15] Hegel's "history as slaughter-bench" is too accurate a characterization of a great deal of human history to justify faith in the present and the likely future, as demonstrated most fundamentally in the prospect of catastrophic climate change.[16]

Reflection on this question, however, can also bring one to advocate and promote the cause of revolution— revolution, as French syndicalist and playwright Albert Camus has it, "for the sake of life," to "give life a chance."[17] A resolution of the climate crisis might be possible through popular disruption of the operations of presently concentrated power.

COP Mindlessness in Cancún

The COP16 negotiations held in the Moon Palace contin- ued the same disastrous pattern of the nearly twenty years of UN-sponsored talks dedicated to addressing the prob- lem of climate change. In an astounding dismissal of recom- mendations made by the IPCC for avoiding a 2°C (3.6°F) increase in average global temperatures beyond those that prevailed in preindustrial times—the end toward which the Cancún Accord itself ineffectually claims to strive—no binding world carbon-reduction trajectory was agreed to at the Cancún COP, nor was any date set for a global peak in carbon emissions. Instead, representatives of powerful states defended existing power and privilege, following the established pattern.

The site of Cancún provided an appropriate back- drop for COP's absurdities. The city, the product of the imagination of Mexican planners some forty years ago, is notable relative to other Mexican cities for the degree to which its lifeworld has been colonized by capital, both national and transnational: installations belonging to Walmart, OXXO, Chedraui, Soriana, and Office Depot blight the built environment in the city center, while a seemingly endless number of hotel monstrosities line the beach of Cancún's *zona hotelera*. Most of these sites have been granted either four- or five-star awards, and hence are completely unaffordable to everyone other than the very privileged. The scale of these installations is gigantic; one hotel in particular models itself after the pyramids of Giza. Located on the supposedly public beaches to which their administrators consciously block off access, these stunning testaments to the social inequality created and overseen by global capitalism stand to be destroyed, like Jimi Hendrix's castles made of sand, by the sea-level rise induced by the melting of the polar ice caps. This sea-level rise is naturally one of the most serious future risks entailed by climate catastrophe. While the destruction of these temples might represent a justified response to the concentration of power and dismissal of human concerns that is practiced by the wealthy and powerful, this sort of resolution could not be had without devastation for large swathes of humanity, two-thirds of which resides in coastal settlements threatened by rising sea levels.[18]

The maintenance and operation of Cancún's luxury hotels and massive corporations is the work of Mexican proletarians. The living conditions of many of these workers—like their counterparts the world over—are lamentable, especially given the contrast of the concentration of wealth exhibited in their places of work. The lot of hotel workers in Cancún calls to mind Marx's comments on capital accumulation: "Accumulation of wealth at one pole is therefore at the same time the accumulation of misery, agony of toil, slavery, ignorance, brutality, [and] mental degradation at the other pole."[19] Whether or not Cancún's proletarians will rise up in defiance, as famously predicted by Marx, is an open question. The seeming lack of participation on the part of locals in mobilizations, discussions, and other events against COP16 proved to be disconcerting, notwithstanding the organizational efforts taken up by various climate activists against this trend.

The master of ceremonies at COP16 was Mexican president Felipe Calderón Hinojosa, from the far-right National Action Party. At one point during COP's two weeks, Calderón was seen literally dressed in green; his major proposal as presented in Cancún was to mandate that the Mexican federal government phase out incandescent bulbs within the country over the next three years.[20] This decidedly minimalist move—one, it should be said, in keeping with the more general trend among the world's states in light of the climate crisis—also was reflected in Calderón's inauguration of a lone wind-energy plant near Cancún on the eve of the summit; the Villa Climática, a space located next to a McDonald's south of the city in which the federal government held exhibits sponsored by Coca-Cola that purportedly examined climate change and hosted a "cultural exhibition" where Nextel, Symantec, Oracle, and other telecommunications corporations were afforded space. The

Villa Climática was catered by, among others, Domino's and Señor Frog's; it also featured a section dedicated to the commemoration of Mexico's bicentennial of formal independence, bearing the title "200 Years of Being Proudly Mexican." No similar space could be found in memory of the Mexican Revolution, the centennial of which was also celebrated in 2010.

COP16 featured a heavy Mexican military and police presence too. One estimate claims there were six thousand units in total at the beginning of the talks.[21] Military patrols in Hummers with machine guns trained on crowds of Cancunenses and outsiders alike were regular events, as was movement by police trucks carrying masked officers with assault rifles. Local news reports in Cancún suggest that the Mexican government acquired a crowd-monitoring drone from the Israeli military.[22] Police and military helicopters originating from the United States could be seen surveilling mobilizations.

In spite of the repressive powers projected in Cancún, though, resistance was also practiced. The international organization Via Campesina put together the Global Forum for Environmental and Social Justice in Cancún's San Jacinto Canek Park to coincide with the second week of COP16. The forum brought six caravans of Mexicans from several regions of the country to report on the socio-environmental situations experienced around the republic, at the end of a year that saw unprecedented rains and attendant flooding in much of southeastern Mexico—a reality for which climate change likely bears responsibility. Via Campesina also invited a number of journalists and other public intellectuals to speak on the climate and socioenvironmental crises, and helped organize a march of approximately three thousand people from central Cancún toward the site of the Moon Palace during COP's second week. The forum was even addressed by Bolivian president Evo Morales, who spoke of the need for a "neosocialism" that incorporates a defense of ecology with class struggle and called for the third millennium to be a "people's millennium," one in which "oligarchy, hierarchy, and monarchy" are overcome as historical residues—however lacking his own leadership has been in these terms for Bolivia itself, particularly in light of the violence exercised by his police in September 2011 against indigenous protesters opposed to the construction of a highway through the highly biodiverse Isiboro Secure National Park.[23]

Apart from Via Campesina's event, Klimaforum10, the successor to Klimaforum09, which at COP15 in Copenhagen released a rather sensible antisystemic analysis of the climate predicament, held an alternative summit on the site of a polo club near Puerto Morelos, a town south of Cancún. Polo players on horseback could be seen some distance from the Klimaforum campus. The summit's site was mirrored in its mainstream politics, which in contrast to those of Klimaforum09, seemed to revolve around inadequate reforms and approaches stressing lifestyle changes to address the environmental crisis. This current was perhaps best symbolized by the talk given at Klimaforum10 by Polly Higgins, a former corporate lawyer from the United Kingdom who argued that what must be done in light of the climate and environmental crises is to codify the crime of ecocide into international law—as though capital respected such law in any sense.[24]

Against approaches that defend existing society through reforms were the perspectives and actions of the revolutionary association known as Anti-C@p in Cancún. An explicitly anticapitalist grouping, Anti-C@p was comprised of autonomous youths hailing largely from Mexico City and connected to Marea Creciente México (Rising Tide Mexico). Anti-C@p's vegetable-oil-powered bus, which also had appeared at the Encounter for Autonomous Life in Oaxaca de Juárez eight months previously, was decorated with murals commemorating the life of Lee Kyung Hae, a Korean agriculturalist who committed suicide in protest of neoliberal capitalism during the World Trade Organization meetings in Cancún in 2003. While tied in ways to Via Campesina's forum against COP, Anti-C@p carried out autonomous actions separate from it. One march organized without a permit by Anti-C@p in the streets of downtown Cancún saw scores of Mexican youths donning Zapatista-style masks and mobilizing with the goal of reaching the local branch of PROFEPA, the Mexican federal government's environmental prosecution agency. Anti-C@p had also planned to disrupt a conference at which Calderón, World Bank president Robert Zoellick, and Walmart CEO Robson Walton were to speak—but it was prevented from doing so due to the police checkpoints erected between the city center and the *zona hotelera*. Indeed, in a spirit of internationalism, during the mobilization called for by Via Campesina during COP's second week, the Anti-C@p bus carried a banner commemorating the two-year anniversary of the murder in Athens of fifteen-year-old Alexandros Grigoropoulos by police. At these and other demonstrations, Anti-C@p presented a spirit of passionate rage against the cruelties of constituted power and the system it upholds—"outbursts of anger in memory of the suffering of [humanity]," as Christos Filippidis characterizes the December 2008 riots in Greece.[25] Similar in this sense to their Greek comrades, and in marked contrast to the other critical currents to be found in Cancún, those associated with Anti-C@p also expressed a degree of sadness with regard to the state of the world. It is unclear whether this intermixing of passions can be considered an expression of the "hopeless sorrow" of which Hegel warns, but it was undoubtedly informed by what Arendt finds to be "the most powerful and perhaps the most devastating passion motivating revolutionaries": "the passion of compassion."[26]

Above all else, human-induced climate change constitutes a brutal assault on humanity and life itself—but with regard to the former, its effects are to be borne overwhelmingly by peoples of the Global South. The drought, famine, flooding, extreme weather events, increased susceptibility to disease, and sea-level rise that follow from climate change will affect human populations residing in southern societies far more severely than those who find themselves in the northern latitudes. While crop yields may well decline some 50 percent over the next ten years on much of the African continent and about 25 percent in Pakistan and Mexico by 2080, parts of Europe and North America stand to enjoy more favorable conditions for agriculture

on average under moderate warming scenarios.[27] In the dry
language of McGill doctoral candidate Jason Samson and
company, global warming can be expected soon to cause
"climate conditions currently associated with high population densities" to "shift towards climate conditions associated with low population densities," in regions determined
by Samson and his colleagues' findings to suffer from high
vulnerability to projected climate change: central South
America, eastern and southern Africa, the Middle East, and
Southeast Asia.[28] In their study of possible future drought
scenarios, geographers Justin Sheffield and Eric Wood
similarly find that southern Africa, West Africa, Central
America, and the Tibetan plateau would be the regions
worst affected by unchecked climate change.[29] Of the three
hundred thousand annual deaths that have been attributed
to human interference with Earth's climate systems to date,
all take place within the "developing world"; 98 percent
of those "seriously affected" by climate change live in such
regions, and an estimated 90 percent of the total economic
losses resulting from climate change are borne by southern
societies.[30] Over 99 percent of the five million who may
well be killed by climate catastrophe in the next decade
reside within societies called "third world."[31]

What is currently occurring, then, is the mass murder of the Global South by much of the Global North.
This trend in world affairs is sadly not without precedent,
given neoliberalism, formal colonization, the Atlantic slave
trade, and the process known as the Columbian Exchange.
Under prevailing assumptions, humanity is little more
than an instrument or object by which to advance capital

accumulation, or else "unpeople" whose interests are to be dismissed entirely.[32] Individuals in general are afforded the same regard as that shown to K. by his murderers at the close of Franz Kafka's *The Trial*, when the protagonist is simply murdered "like a dog."

Prevailing society's relationship to the climate predicament can be described as upholding a sort of climate barbarism reminiscent of fascism. Fascism—the violent defense of authoritarian social structures, maintained by the silencing of suffering—is hardly the exclusive mantle of the Nazis, Benito Mussolini, Francisco Franco, or imperial Japan. In the view of Tunisian anticolonial theorist Alberto Memmi, fascism refers to "a regime of oppression for the benefit of a few."[33] On Arendt's account, totalitarianism originated precisely from imperialist liberalism; for Marcuse, the "total-authoritarian state" is the form that corresponds to the monopoly stage of capitalism, to which liberal capitalism inevitably gives rise.[34] As Horkheimer argues, "They have nothing to say about fascism who do not want to mention capitalism."[35] The stubborn refusal by those in power to commit to mitigating future climate change and making resources available for humanity's materially impoverished societies to attempt to adapt to the destruction wrought by climate change amounts to collaboration with the future death of a decidedly overwhelming number of human beings on a scale far greater than any other in human history. In this is seen the irrationality and barbarism of capitalism—its total authoritarianism. Given that present climate change has been observed to be contingent on the rise and perpetuation of the capitalist system, deaths due to climate destabilization would result not from "natural" causes but rather human-induced ones, and should be considered homicides. Humanity thus "waits to be woken one day by the memory of what has been lost"—principally, the three hundred thousand individuals currently killed each year by capital-induced climate change, and a sum that could well rise to a million annual deaths within the near future if matters are not radically changed.[36]

As Marx insists, shame can be a revolutionary virtue.[37] Shame regarding humanity's marked failures to protect itself along with the other forms of life with which it shares Earth could help contribute to the radical reconstruction of global society—for this society, though ruled over by the repressive order of statist militarism, is "after all constituted out of us," Adorno observes, "made up of us ourselves."[38]

The response of the world's peoples to the massive suffering brought about by climate change—dramatically illustrated, for example, in the extreme devastation seen in the 2011 "children's famine" in the Horn of Africa, which has caused tens of thousands of deaths and imperiled the lives of millions, mainly in Somalia—must not ape that of the old manservant at the close of the *The Misunderstanding* by Camus. In Camus's work, the character Maria, having just learned of her husband's murder at the hands of the servant's managers, desperately asks him to aid her, to "be kind and say that you will help me": his response is a rather pointed "No."[39]

Among many other considerations, the problem of climate change raises serious questions about the place of progress in

history. "However passionately we may desire the elimina-
tion of fascism," asserts German Marxist Franz Neumann,
"we cannot close our eyes to the possibility that it may not
be wiped out."[40] The many horrors promised by climate
change, with their potentially fascist implications, may well
not be prevented and averted. It is hardly inconceivable that
the present course toward a climate-devastated Earth will
not be arrested and radically redirected. While human history would have likely fared far better were it not subjected
to events such as European colonialism, World War I, or
the invention and proliferation of nuclear weapons, the fact
of the matter is that such horrors did in fact come about.
The "astonishment" Walter Benjamin notes in the realization that "the things we are experiencing in the 20th [or
21st] century are *still* possible" is tenable only if one sub-
scribes to philosophical orientations that see, like Hegel, the
steady march of progress in the passage of historical time.[41]
In words written by journalist Ulrike Meinhof before her
questionable collaboration with the Red Army Faction,
"Recognizing that something is unreasonable does not necessarily mean it will not happen. There has already been a
time in Germany when people thought 'This can't be true,'
and it was true, and cost millions of them their lives."[42]

Adorno writes that "there is horror because there is no
freedom yet."[43] The Chinese Marxist economist Minqi Li is
correct to note that "there is no hope whatsoever to achieve
climate stabilization so long as the world is organized as
a system that is based on production for profit and struc-
tured to pursue endless capital accumulation."[44] Against this
radical lack that characterizes the forms in which humanity

is at present entrapped nonetheless stands the chance for what French aesthetician Maurice Merleau-Ponty calls the "advent of humanity," or what Adorno terms "a rational establishment of overall society as humankind"—a possibility that in the latter's view "opens in the face of extinction."[45] Global human society must come to "abandon blood and horror," both as an intrinsic and instrumental end, for the "debarbarization of humanity is the immediate prerequisite for survival."[46]

Fortunately for our prospects, humanity has long resisted. The revolt of the Helots against Sparta as well as the slave rebellions led by Spartacus and Toussaint L'Ouverture are in ways continued in modern times by the efforts of the Spanish anarchists, the anti-Nazi resistance, the Ejército Zapatista de Liberación Nacional (EZLN), the Naxalites of eastern and central India, and the Movement for the Emancipation of the Niger Delta, among other groups and collectives. This tradition, advanced in Cancún by Anti-C@p, involves "resistance of the eye that does not want the colors of the world to fade."[47] It has been continued by activists in recent years through, for example, the attempted shutdown of the city of San Francisco the day after the commencement of the March 2003 invasion of Iraq, the blockading of an Israeli air base during the July 2006 war on southern Lebanon, the "decommissioning" of an EDO MBM weapons production plant in the United Kingdom in January 2009, the direct actions to defend and liberate oppressed nonhuman animals, the antagonistic fury expressed in Greece against the state and capital in December 2008, the destruction of police stations in Egypt and popular storming of the Israeli embassy in Cairo, and the peoples' rebellions that have gripped much of the Arab world since December 2010, in addition to the popular occupations of public space that have followed in many Western societies.

As can readily be seen through reflection on the fate to date of these revolts, though—and generally on the "failed culture" that has allowed for genocide, the possibility of nuclear warfare, and potentially catastrophic climate change—the specter of despair is far from illusory. While it is to be hoped, as Egyptian Marxist Samir Amin suggests, that the recent waves of popular revolt against oligarchy and tyranny will amount to the "autumn for capitalism and the springtime for the peoples of the South"—or that, as world-systems theorist Immanuel Wallerstein writes, the global protest movement of 2011 will carry the revolutionary "1968 current" into the future—the outcome remains uncertain.[48] An orthodox Marxist faith that the subordinated necessarily will be victorious in history—that the abolition of capitalism follows from "the premises now in existence"—cannot itself be justified.[49] On the contrary, the fear Adorno observes in Marx regarding a "relapse into barbarism" is a rational one, considering that "the relapse has already occurred."[50]

In light of the problems posed by the threat of capital-induced climate destabilization, it remains clear that if humanity does not "determine itself," it will "bring about terrestrial catastrophe."[51] The dark choice presently faced by humankind, in the prognosis of Belgian Situationist Raoul Vaneigem, is that of suicide or revolution.[52]

Contemplation of this choice is the task of the remainder of this work, which investigates past catastrophes, synthesizes current climatological findings, and considers the question of hope for a "progress that leads out and away" from total negation.[53]

Against the dominion of death, it is to be the position expressed in this book, as Arendt declares beautifully in a repudiation of the philosophy advanced by her mentor Martin Heidegger, that humans, "though they must die, are not born in order to die but in order to begin."[54]

The Death of Life?

One wants to break free from the past: rightly, because nothing at all can live in its shadow . . . ; wrongly, because the past that one would like to evade is still very much alive.

—Theodor W. Adorno, "The Meaning of Working through the Past"

Reflecting in *Remnants of Auschwitz*, Italian political theorist Giorgio Agamben notes that "human beings are human insofar as they bear witness to the inhuman."[1] Besides the value of such a perspective as regards the particularity of the Nazi genocide of European Jews as well as other serious historical crimes, such a consideration could be helpful in terms of the current predicament, for an examination of the degree of inhumanity threatened by prevailing society could perhaps aid humanity in protecting itself against a general lapse into barbarism.

In what follows, climate catastrophe is compared with the horror posed by nuclear conflagration—a horror that is hardly a mere historical one. U.S. antinuclear writer Jonathan Schell's *The Fate of the Earth* (1982) and *The Abolition* (1984) are used to navigate this exploration. While world-renowned anarchist philosopher Noam Chomsky is right to state that it is "not pleasant to speculate about the likely consequences if concentrated power continues on its present course," it is also true that the chance for overcoming brutality and unreason can be helped along by critical inquiry, as Chomsky often stresses.[2]

The central question examined in Schell's *The Fate of the Earth* and *The Abolition* is the implications raised by the existence of nuclear weapons in relation to Earth's very habitability. The mere existence of such weapons threatens the "murder of the future," in Schell's words.[3] In a world imperiled by the factual existence of nuclear arms, the primary responsibility is to reverse the conditions that threaten human survival, because there can self-evidently be no value without human existence, as Schell rightly argues. Just as the right to food is "the first right," as utopian socialist Charles Fourier asserts—one that underpins all others—human survival is a precondition for all aspects of human social life, not least of these the very "self reflection" Adorno finds to be necessary for the protection of survival itself.[4]

Schell's harrowing account of nuclear annihilation places future generations, whose potential existence would quite simply be canceled by the death of humanity resulting from nuclear holocaust, at the center of concern. Voiceless and disregarded, future generations thus share much with the nonhuman world and ecosphere, generally understood. Schell movingly expresses the gravity of the situation faced by a nuclear-armed humanity in his reflections on Arendt's notion of natality—the various beginnings made possible by life. He writes that the annihilation risked by nuclear weapons threatens the "root of life, the spring from which life arises": birth, or the "power of communities composed of mortal beings to regenerate and preserve themselves in history." Clearly, such a predicament is far more serious than that posed by individual death, for extinction, in threatening natality, jeopardizes "the continuation of the world in which all our common enterprises occur and have their meaning."[5]

The threat of extinction for Schell is a systemic evil. It follows the legacy of terror and genocide as practiced by the Nazis and other fascist forces—including as a matter of course the U.S. government, the first and only force to have directly employed nuclear weapons against human populations. The existence of these weapons jeopardizes, in the first place, the lives of billions of human beings and the very underpinnings of global human society, but their being also threatens a total assault on Earth's systems taken as a whole. Nuclear arms in this sense amount to the single most advanced weapon in humanity's general assault on nature. Given that the support systems allowing for the biological existence of the millions of species on Earth would essentially be dismantled by a war involving nuclear arms—that is, a possibility that follows from the very existence of such arms— a nuclear-devastated planet Earth would be capable of supporting only radically simplified life-forms, if any life at all is to survive such an event. Indeed, the extent of human knowledge regarding the effects that can be expected from the hypothetical future event of nuclear war is both vast and alarming, says Schell.[6]

In light of the knowledge available to humans regarding the risks implied by the development and possession of nuclear weapons, the lack of conscious action on humanity's part designed to resolve the problem of nuclear weapons—abolition—is to Schell a manifestation of social insanity. At times mirroring the critiques of social democracy and other reformist political philosophies raised by Benjamin and others, Schell writes with concern on the tendency to repress reflection on the existence of nuclear weapons. The "normality" sought by ideologies and practices that distract from as well as actively subvert the project of resolving the nuclear threat is in this sense "mass insanity," since it defends the iron cage that has "quietly grown up around the earth, imprisoning every person on it." Statist nuclear policy, which seeks to prevent the employment of nuclear weapons by threatening total destruction of a would-be nuclear aggressor by means of nuclear weapons, is drastically bereft of reason, as its effectiveness results precisely from its stated commitment to bringing about nuclear hostilities—an eventuality that could well end in nuclear annihilation. Such a development would be self-evidently absurd and totally unjust. As the destruction of humanity can never be an ethical act—for the drowning of "all human purposes" for "all time" would be the supreme negation of ethical action—it follows that no justification can be had for postures and acts that threaten humanity's collective suicide by means of nuclear annihilation—conditions that rationally can be expected to "transform the world into a desert," as Arendt fears, and thus deliver what German philosopher Günther Anders terms "sheer nothingness": a "rotating globe without any life on it."[7] That humanity in fact came to endanger itself through the invention, development, and maintenance of nuclear arms constitutes, in Schell's view, the "greatest collective failure of responsibility by any generation in history." Under such conditions, "self-congratulation is certainly out of order," however much people in general may seem to have adjusted to and accepted the monstrousness implied in the threat nuclear weapons hold for life.[8]

The political arrangements Schell analyzes, then, threaten the institution of what he terms the "absolute and eternal darkness" of human extinction.[9] Were there to be a nuclear war, no escape would be possible; that a given society were consciously to have elected to ban nuclear weapons within its territory, for example, would matter little for its fate in light of the possibility of nuclear annihilation originating elsewhere. Under such conditions, writes Schell, there is within the corridors of power "no one to speak for man [sic] and for the earth," even if both are threatened with destruction.[10] As P. D. James has her character Theo in The Children of Men lament, it would seem that there exists "no security or home for [our] endangered species anywhere under the uncaring sky."[11]

For Schell, the prospect of resolving the terminal threat posed by nuclear destruction can begin only through reflection on this very question—a process likely serving as the basis for his *The Fate of the Earth* and *The Abolition*. A means to "salvation" could be made possible if humanity were to "permit [itself] to recognize clearly the breadth and depth of the peril—to assure [itself] once and for all of its boundlessness and durability," for if the profundity of the threat were to be generally acknowledged, consideration of the "peril of self-extinction" could take the place Schell claims it deserves within our conceptions of being—that is to say, central. Humans may of course choose to "ignore the peril," though such a position would be patently absurd and grossly irresponsible, writes Schell, given the "danger of imminent self-destruction." Echoing Marcuse, Schell notes that it is necessary for the possibility of nuclear annihilation to repress any contemplation of the "magnitude and significance of the peril," since the means that threaten this end can persist only if humanity in general fails to understand the nuclear predicament and act accordingly. The possibility of extinction, then, arises through the dominance of modes of thinking about the problem that "at least partly deflec[t] our attention from what it is."[12]

Far from subscribing to philosophical idealism, Schell hardly considers the threat of humanity's collective suicide at the hands of nuclear weapons just "something to contemplate." He emphasizes that it is instead "something to rebel against" and ultimately defeat. On his account, recognition of the peril posed by nuclear weapons could in concrete terms lead first to the development of a subject that could carry out the abolition of nuclear weapons and second to the reorganization of global human society along lines that would minimize the chance that they be constructed again. Humanity in this sense is called to break with the "resignation and acceptance" with which many persons approach individual death, and come to engage in "arousal, rejection, indignation, and action" aimed at overthrowing the threat of the death of the species by means of nuclear self-destruction.[13]

Despite the enormity of the problem, overthrowing existing social relations is in fact a possibility, claims Schell. It is still possible for humanity to prevail in this sense, on Schell's account, though the abolition of the threat of nuclear annihilation would demand thoroughgoing socio-political change of an unprecedented scale. The chance for such change could begin only through recognizing that the world's prevailing modes of political organization, in failing to resolve the very real threat posed to life by nuclear weapons, are in "drastic need of replacement."[14] In place of the exercise of statecraft, people would "reinvent" politics and "reinvent" the world.[15] The action of a self-conscious humanity would institute the principle whereby humans have no right to destroy the "earthly creation on which everyone depends for survival" and would overturn the despair that prevails under conditions in which hope for survival is itself jeopardized. Against the remarkable lack of action on the part of constituted power to ensure survival, then, humanity in general could counterpose a "worldwide program of action for preserving the species." Such an end demands that the "politics of the earth" be "revolutionize[d]," for only a "revolution in thought and in action" will allow for survival. The choice for Schell is quite simply "extinction" or "global political revolution": "Our present system and the institutions that make it up are the debris of history. They have become inimical to life, and must be swept away. They constitute a noose around the neck of mankind [*sic*], threatening to choke off the human future, but we can cut the noose and break free." Humans in this sense are called to become "partners in the protection of life itself" rather than the "allies of death." Schell envisions "all human beings" coming together to "join in a defensive alliance, with nuclear weapons as their common enemy."[16]

Schell's concern in *The Fate of the Earth* and *The Abolition* is not exactly to explore the possible nature of such a conscious political movement, but he does at times make fragmentary comments regarding it. For him, the imperative of survival demands that each person take on a "share of the responsibility for guaranteeing the existence of all future generations." The institution of action motivated by such maxims would establish a "new relationship among human beings"—one basing itself in a sociable responsibility for others. Indeed, Schell writes that the "first principle" of the movement on the part of a conscious humanity in defense of life would be "respect for human beings, born and unborn, based on our common love of life and our common jeopardy in the face of our own destructive powers and inclinations."[17]

In Kantian terms, no human being, whether currently existing or rationally expected to come into life in the future, would be "regarded as an auxiliary" within the new political world to be fashioned by conscious opponents of extinction. Radical exclusion, that is, would be a reality to overcome in the bringing about of an Earth liberated from nuclear weapons. This point is particularly relevant to a consideration of the fate of potential future generations, whose very future birth is imperiled by nuclear weapons. "Love," in Schell's view, "can enable them to be," by resolving the arrangements that threaten to "shut [them] up in nothingness" forever.[18]

According to Schell, the abolition of the state form is central to the task of resisting the total darkness of nuclear annihilation. Those societies that possess nuclear weapons have placed a "higher value on national sovereignty" than on human survival, writes Schell, as they are "ultimately prepared to bring an end to [humanity] in their attempt to protect their own countries." In a real way, the threat of extinction follows from the division of the world's peoples and territories into sovereign states, for the state and its war-making capacities have been preserved even following the advent of nuclear arms, at the cost of all human life. The alternative to such death as proposed by Schell is that the world's states relinquish their sovereignty, destroy nuclear weapons, dismantle offensive military capabilities, and establish a global political system in which violence has ceased to be the final arbiter.[19]

Prior to a look at current climatological findings, some commentary on Schell's views as presented here is in order. The similarities between Schell's account of the threat of nuclear annihilation and the present climate predicament should be fairly clear, since they are "two of a kind," as Schell himself recognizes in a January 2010 interview.[20] The perpetuation of dangerous human interference with Earth's climate systems, like the prospect of nuclear war, would be "irredeemably senseless," and may even threaten oblivion for humanity.[21] If we are to attempt to even begin resolving the threats posed by climate change and nuclear arms—if we are to avoid becoming "the allies of death" and "under-writers of the slaughter of billions of innocent people"—we must rebel with the aim of overthrowing that which exists, as Schell and other commentators rightly note—and as our own reason and conscience would demand.[22]

Besides the justified urgency that motivates Schell's works, much of the commentary he makes on the socio-political implications of the nuclear arms problem bears consideration. It is the historical division of the world into sovereign states that raises the threat of nuclear annihila-tion in the first place, and it is the perpetuation of this state system that defends the capitalist mode of produc-tion threatening climate catastrophe. "The state of death is identical to that of sovereignty," Benjamin writes—or at least it threatens to be so.[23] The nuclear danger continues to exist as long as nuclear weapons and the states that protect them exist too; as Chomsky observes, it has effectively been a "miracle" that nuclear arms have not again been directly employed against persons since their first use in August 1945.[24] Similarly, the threat of irradiation of the biosphere that would follow from the related problem of a full-blown meltdown at any one of the hundreds of the world's nuclear energy plants lives on, as the 2011 disaster at the Fukushima-Daichi site reminds us. This risk persists insofar as such technologies are generally found to be acceptable.

Considerations regarding human vulnerability to these various threats have guided popular mobilizations in opposition to technological madness in antinuclear movements past and present. This movement from below—*desde abajo y a la izquierda* ("from below and to the left"), as the neo-Zapatistas put it—would do well to heed Schell's call for an association to overthrow social exclusion, both for the presently suffering social majorities and the expected future generations, and in so doing, institute a political act of love and respect. Particularly important for this end, as Schell contends, is the task of examining the depth of the peril and the darkness it promises. To contemplate recent climatological findings on the current and possible future state of Earth's climate systems is to confirm Benjamin's diagnosis of the prevailing state of affairs as amounting to an emergency that demands revolutionary resolution.

The Breadth of Climate Barbarism

> The need to lend suffering a voice is a condition for all truth.
>
> —Theodor W. Adorno, *Negative Dialectics*

In the estimation of world-renowned NASA climatologist James Hansen, "Planet Earth . . . is in imminent peril," is "in imminent danger of crashing," precisely because of the dangerous interference since the rise of industrial capitalism by the West and its followers with Earth's climate systems.[25] This interference—driven primarily by the use of fossil fuels, which in turn have driven economic expansion and attendant explosions of social inequality since the origins of modernity—has caused the atmospheric carbon dioxide (CO_2) concentration to rise from a preindustrial level of 280 ppm to the present 394 ppm. Due to the heat-trapping characteristics of atmospheric CO_2, average global temperatures have risen an estimated 0.8°C (1.4°F) since preindustrial times. Because a time lapse of some decades exists between the point at which hydrocarbons are released into the environment and the point at which they in fact contribute to global warming, a great deal more warming can be expected based solely on the emissions that have been caused to date—at least 1.4°C (2.45°F) over preindustrial average global temperature levels, according to one estimate.[26] The Nobel Prize–winning IPCC estimates in its 2007 Fourth Annual Report that global average temperatures could rise by a total of between 1.1°C and 6.4°C (1.93°F–11.2°F) by the end of this century—though as some commentators disconcertingly note, such predictions may constitute significant underestimates, considering that the various feedback mechanisms that might turn climate change into a self-perpetuating phenomenon—discussed below—are still unquantified and hence excluded from the data on which the IPCC bases its conclusions.[27] Hansen, for one, insists that the global atmospheric carbon concentration must be reduced to no more than 350 ppm, "if humanity wishes to preserve a planet similar to that on which civilization is based."[28] Australian environmentalists David Spratt and Philip Sutton recommend an even more radical target of 315 ppm, which they associate with an average increase of only 0.5°C (0.88°F) over the temperature that prevailed in preindustrial human history—a goal similar to that endorsed at the April 2010 World People's Conference on Climate Change and the Rights of Mother Earth held by the Morales government in Cochabamba.[29]

The average global temperature increase of 0.8°C (1.4°F) observed to date has already profoundly affected many of Earth's peoples and much of the planet itself. While mainstream U.S. media has frantically sought to cast doubt on the responsibility that the warming experienced until now has had for the marked increase in the frequency and destructiveness of recent extreme weather events, a number of climatologists are alleging that such skepticism is unwarranted, in a marked reversal of the reluctance with which many climate researchers have so far approached this question.[30]

Turning to the devastation for which capital-induced climate catastrophe is responsible, some 20 million residents of Pakistan, for instance, were displaced by the unprecedented flooding in summer 2010 that destroyed some 1.2 million homes, killed 1,600 people, and injured over 2,300 others, leaving between one-fifth and one-third of the state's cultivated farmland temporarily submerged.[31] When the floodwaters receded from Pakistan's central province of Punjab, silt deposits were left behind, covering large swathes of land previously dedicated to agricultural production.[32] A United Nations Children's Fund report from September 2010 warned that more than 100,000 Pakistani children were at risk of dying of malnutrition over the subsequent six months because of the floods.[33] A follow-up report in early

2011 found that about one-quarter of the children in the Sindh Province were malnourished, with 6 percent "severely underfed"—rates analogous to those observed in African famines.[34] Flooding in Pakistan in summer 2011, while less apocalyptically disastrous than the preceding year, nonetheless destroyed 100,000 homes, inundated 900 villages, and displaced an estimated 5 million people.[35]

Climate change has been deemed directly responsible, because local scientists have found that warming has steadily shifted monsoon rains to the northwestern regions of Pakistan over the past four decades, away from the larger rivers more capable of absorbing significant rains.[36] Everything else being equal, moreover, a warmer atmosphere can also be expected to produce more violent precipitation events such as these, as warmer air holds more water vapor than does colder air.[37] That constituted power has failed to provide the resources needed for some sort of adequate reconstruction of Pakistan after the floods—that some 8 million affected people lacked basic health care, food, shelter, and schooling a year after the disaster—is entirely unsurprising, however grave the implications for human welfare.[38]

Shifting to the continent of Africa, 2010 also saw the emergence of famine conditions that jeopardized the lives of approximately 10 million residents of Africa's Sahel region—principally the countries of Niger, Chad, Mali, and Mauritania—as rains failed for a second consecutive year, causing the annual "lean season" between the running down of food stocks and harvest season to come three months earlier than usual.[39] Oxfam representative Caroline

Gluck compared the social devastation induced by the famine conditions in Niger to suffering caused by the 1984–85 famine in Ethiopia, which killed 1 million people.[40] As was the case with a similarly severe food crisis that gripped the Sahel in 2005, it is unknown precisely how many actually lost their lives, but an estimated 400,000 children were expected to die from starvation in the months following June 2010 without an appropriate relief response.[41]

Fire conflagrations experienced in much of central Russia in 2010 led to the death of an estimated 56,000 people and destroyed an estimated one-fourth of the country's arable land, leading Prime Minister Vladimir Putin to declare an indefinite moratorium on grain exportation from Russia, the world's fourth-largest grain exporter, with serious consequences for food prices—and hence, people's ability to feed themselves—in importer countries.[42] Those worst affected in this sense reside in Afghanistan, Burundi, the Democratic Republic of Congo, Sudan, Eritrea, and Ethiopia, among other impoverished states.[43] Heat waves were to blame for unprecedented temperatures in South Asia in May and June 2010—53.7°C (128.6°F) at the ruins of Mohenjo-Daro in Pakistan in early June—that killed thousands, though it is unclear if the death toll from these events approached that of Europe in summer 2003, when some 35,000 people succumbed to heat-induced death.[44] The UN Global Disaster Alert and Coordination System dubbed the flooding caused by torrential rains in Sri Lanka in late 2010 and early 2011 a once-in-a-century event; the rains washed away 80 percent of the rice crop on the island country's eastern Batticaloa district.[45] Additionally, 2010 saw a drought in Amazonia the likes of which had not been experienced for some forty years, with the Rio Negro, one of the Amazon's largest tributaries, reduced to its lowest levels since records began in 1902 and an estimated eight gigatons of CO_2 emitted by dying trees—a greater total amount, it should be added, than the estimated present annual carbon emissions of China, the greatest current emitter of all.[46] In the Arctic, an ice island four times the size of Manhattan broke off Greenland's Petermann glacier in August of the same year; indeed, the 2010 Arctic summer ice extent was the third-lowest ever recorded, and the same data for 2011 may well match the all-time low observed in 2007—reflections of the "death spiral" into which the Arctic ice has been forced.[47]

Climate change likely also bears responsibility for the disastrous flooding experienced in the U.S. South in mid-2011 and Hurricane Irene that same summer as well as the dry spring in northern Europe and the southwestern United States—the former having brought about the driest April observed since people started keeping records in England in the seventeenth century, and the latter the driest spring in more than a century.[48] Climate overheating is also the likely culprit for the spectacular drought suffered in China in 2011, which drove Chinese authorities to release some five billion cubic meters of water from behind the infamous Three Gorges Dam for irrigation and personal use.[49] Anthropogenic interference with Earth's climate systems is clearly seen as well in the catastrophic failure of rains in the Horn of Africa in 2011 and the attendant drought, found by the United Nations to be the worst in six decades.[50] This devastating event left some 13 million individuals at risk of dying from starvation—a number that included millions of children, thousands of whom have perished to date.[51] It is this event, together with the ongoing torturous civil conflict in the region, that has seen thousands of desperate Somalis arriving daily at the Dadaab refugee camp in Kenya, a settlement originally established two decades ago to house 90,000 persons, but now populated by some 500,000; it is this event that has brought about the conditions for the emergence of malnutrition rates of 58 percent among children in Somalia's Bay region, and thus the potential death of three-quarters of a million people, as the United Nations warns.[52]

These disconcerting events have taken place in just the past two years. In addition to the 2003 heat waves in Europe, episodes of drought in western North America (1994–2004) and Central and Southwest Asia (1998–2003) along with flooding in Europe (2002) are "consistent," in the IPCC's words, with "physically based expectations arising from climate change."[53] It is estimated that China loses 965 square miles to desertification annually; increased sea levels have already begun to sterilize the soils of Tuvalu and the Solomon Islands, hampering the cultivation of taro in both island groups.[54] In Kiribati, rising sea levels are salinizing the water supplies; on Vietnam's Mekong Delta rivers, they are forcing agriculturists to abandon rice cultivation en masse.[55] Lake Chad in the Sahel has been reduced to 10 percent of its size only forty years ago, and Lake Tanganyika was observed in mid-2010 to have higher temperatures than at any other time in the past fifteen hundred years and is warming at an unprecedented rate.[56] The world's oceans are 30 percent more acidic now than a century ago.[57] Glaciers across the globe are in steady retreat, with 75 percent of the Himalayan glaciers now classified this way according to a March 2011 study.[58] Temperatures observed in Tibet in 2010 reached highs not previously seen in the past five decades of record keeping.[59] Peru's glaciers have lost 22 percent of their surface area over the past few decades.[60]

Oxfam reports that flooding and extreme storm disaster events have tripled in impoverished southern societies since the 1980s.[61] As Edward S. Herman and David Peterson note, the genocidal conflict in Darfur may have found some of its basis in the climate change that has already occurred.[62] A recent Columbia University study found that historical conflict in southern societies were twice as likely in years with an active El Niño Southern Oscillation, which in drastically decreasing rainfall patterns over much of the tropics—Africa, the Middle East, India, and Southeast Asia—simulate the conditions that further climate destabilization can be expected to bring about.[63] Mike Davis's findings that the historical synergy between late nineteenth-century El Niño events and the onset of capitalist colonialism in India, China, and much of Africa produced the worst famines recorded in human history—ones that killed between 30 and 60 million people—take on new meaning in light of today's climate change.[64]

To date, then, climate change has proven disastrous, yet the threats posed by climate destabilization will likely be far more severe in the near future. The following examines some of the climatological findings regarding our downward spiral toward climate catastrophe—an eventuality that is promised without a rational and revolutionary intervention to check it.

In its 2007 Fourth Annual Report, the IPCC offers its worst-case scenario of a 6.4°C (11.2°F) increase in average temperatures by the end of the twenty-first century as being based on the lack of any sort of sensible mitigating policies and the reproduction of fossil-fuel-intensive capitalist growth. The report states that a 2°C (3.6°F) increase in average temperatures is associated with an atmospheric carbon concentration of about 500 ppm, a 3°C (5.25°F) rise with 600 ppm, and a 5°C–6°C (8.75–11.2°F) increase with 900–1,000 ppm.[65] As has already been noted, humanity presently finds itself tied to a trajectory that would see the realization of this 6°C increase by the century's end. The UK Met Office maintains that a 4°C (7°F) increase by the year 2060 is entirely possible. Anderson's predictions for life in a world warmer by 4°C, mentioned above, is relevant here, as is Hansen and his colleagues' determination that the current warming rate is progressing between ten and a thousand times more rapidly than the nearly terminal extinction rate at the end of the end of the Permian era.[66]

At lower levels of climate change (1°C–2°C), say climatological reports, much of the world's oceans will be rendered dangerously acidic due to the mass dissolving of CO_2 in water, the subtropical arid belt that currently rests where the Sahara lies will likely move into southern Europe, India's wheat-producing northern states will be devastated, the Andes' glacial ice could well disappear altogether, and the critical melt threshold for the Greenland ice sheet will have been surpassed.[67] Regions of

China face significantly higher vulnerability to parasitic disease given a 2°C (3.6°F) global temperature increase, and the general incidence of diarrheal diseases will likely increase significantly under such conditions.[68] Drought and desertification from such warming levels will increase the probability that little food will be available on the international markets; mass starvation is thus to be expected.[69] With a 3°C (5.25°F) increase, the sand seas of the Kalahari Desert are expected to begin expanding, thereby rendering Botswana and much of the rest of southern Africa uninhabitable by humans; much of Central America and Australia will no longer be able to support agricultural production; Amazonia will likely collapse into a desert of Saharan proportions; and a permanent El Niño would be instituted.[70] Citing his colleague David Archer, German climatologist Hans Joachim Schellnhuber asserts that a 2°C–3°C increase in average global temperatures could provoke a sea-level rise of 164 feet (50 meters).[71] With a 4°C–5°C temperature increase, agriculture would be abandoned throughout much of the world, with devastating increases in mortality. This destruction of agriculture would result not just from overheating, increased evaporation rates, and decreased rainfall rates, but also by the intrusion of saltwater into aquifers used for agricultural purposes, as follows from rising sea levels.[72] The terrestrial conflagration seen even in a world 2°C warmer than preindustrial levels would itself be accelerated and exacerbated by the release of the estimated 1.5 trillion tons of carbon presently trapped in the Arctic permafrost. A mid-2011 study found that the

catastrophic, entirely irreversible potential mass release
of permafrost could well transpire within two decades.[73]
Russian authorities have recently announced that their
country's permafrost regions could well shrink by 30
percent before midcentury.[74]

Of perhaps all climatological findings, research on the
positive feedback loops that are being induced by warming is the most frightening: the increased absorption of
solar radiation that results from reduced deflection by
disappearing glacial white surfaces, higher frequency and
intensity of forest fires, worsening oceanic acidification,
and permafrost and methane release unleashed by overheating would cause warming trends to generate their own
momentum toward even hotter states. A 2009 study on
climate change performed at the Massachusetts Institute
of Technology—less optimistic and thus perhaps more
realistic, for example, than the IPCC's reports to date regarding the prospect of achieving significant carbon emission reductions in the near future—finds there indeed to
be a chance that temperatures will increase 7.4°C (13°F)
over preindustrial temperatures by the century's end,
with a 90 percent chance that the temperature increase
would range between 3.5°C and 7.4°C (4.8°F–13°F).[75]
The study's authors are quick to clarify that even their
decidedly bleak conclusions might be underestimates, as
they, like the IPCC, do not fully account for the various
feedback mechanisms that could arise given catastrophic
climate change. NASA's Dennis Bushnell, for his part,
estimates that the average global temperature increase
expected during this century once these feedbacks have

been accounted for would amount to between 6°C and 12°C (10.5°F–21°F).[76] Warming of such apocalyptic proportions would be entirely horrific: it should be remembered that it was a 6°C (10.5°F) increase that triggered the end-Permian mass extinction.[77]

Though a matter of controversy among climatologists, there is reason to fear that overheating beyond these levels could induce a runaway greenhouse effect that would give rise to what Hansen terms "the Venus syndrome," whereby climatic change abruptly delivers Earth to a state resembling that of Venus, where life simply cannot exist.[78]

Fragmentary Critique

Nature as Possibility

The beauty that is to be found throughout much of the life-world points to a "beyond," a radically other lived experience. The experience of beauty thus displaces the everyday world, similar in this sense to the experience of interpersonal love. Nature can also be seen as "a subject with which to live."[1] As Adorno writes, natural beauty "recollects a world without domination."[2] It militates radically against the world that has been reduced to "a gigantic gasoline station" in favor of a totality that overthrows "the evil senselessly visited" on "all the persecuted, whether animals or human beings."[3]

Against Forgetting

Reflecting on nature can help people remember their origins, for humanity itself arose from nature. Humans are not aliens that chanced on Earth; they came about through coevolution with other beings, however destructive their present relationships. Anyone familiar with the genetic similarity between humans and particular apes, or who has ever observed a chimpanzee infant, is familiar with the continuum of evolution of which humans are a part—a point rightly stressed by animal rights theorist Steven Best.[4] These commonalities might be a potential basis for solidarity among species, and particularly for the human abolition of the practice of speciesism.

Ethology, the study of different ape species, has been seminal to the human understanding of self and other. While its demonstration of the similarities among the different species of the primate order should lend itself to concern for and sensitivity among humans toward other animals, it does not follow that primate ethology necessarily advances liberatory perspectives—just as considerations of the even higher rates of genetic similarity among humans themselves has hardly put an end to interhuman oppression. Through highlighting the violent, hierarchical behavior engaged in by given chimpanzee groupings, anthropologist Christopher Boehm, for one, attempts to show that the human race is doomed to a similar fate precisely due to the biological similarities between the two species.[5] For commentator Elise Boulding, though, humans have the capacity to behave less like chimpanzees and baboons, and more like the "unaggressive, vegetarian, food-sharing" gibbon, who also has fathers "as much involved in child-rearing as mother[s]."[6] It is perhaps heartening that Friedrich Engels claims that the first humans—those at the "lower stage" of "savagery," or the first of three historical-developmental stages identified by Engels and Lewis Henry Morgan before him—consumed nothing more than "fruits, nuts, and roots."[7] Such considerations, taken together with many others, may give credence to Marcuse's claim that only at a later, contingent point of humanity's historical development does "an essentially aggressive, offensive subject, whose thoughts and actions [are] designed for mastering objects," emerge.[8] And in this we may perhaps discover a sense of the importance of Adorno and Horkheimer's injunction to remember nature, the very origin of humankind.[9]

For Cooperation

Adorno is somewhat mistaken in his assertion that human history "continues the unconscious history of nature, of devouring and being devoured."[10] While human society surely apes the thoughtless violence experienced throughout much of the nonhuman world, it cannot so quickly be said that all of nature itself perpetuates this dynamic. Adorno's claim overlooks the numerous herbivore species that have arisen through the processes of evolution. In addition, it ignores the very real cooperation engaged in by members of species with species members, as well as members of other species. This factor has shaped evolution at least as much as Darwinian struggle, as anarchist biologist Peter Kropotkin's work *Mutual Aid* shows.[11]

On Climate Refugees

The French Collectif Argos's 2007 volume *Réfugiés climatiques* (*Climate Refugees*) is a series of essays and sets of photographs that examine the lives of a number of social groups of people from around the globe who have been or likely soon will be victimized by climate change. The work itself is proof of massive human rights violations, whether past or possible future, as well as the stunning destruction of ethnodiversity that climate catastrophe threatens to bring about. Though much of its textual argumentation is allied to reformism, its coverage of a number of regions in which individuals are menaced by climate change—the Arctic, Bangladesh, Chad, the Maldives Islands, the U.S. Gulf Coast, northern Germany, Tuvalu, northern China, and Nepal—is crucial; moreover, many of its photos are certainly worthy of reflection.

Yet *Réfugiés climatiques*'s written reflections on the prospect of climate catastrophe are disappointingly tame—perhaps the product of a reliance on the now-outdated climatological reports available when the work was written. One of the book's introductory essays, by Jean Jouzel, a high-ranking IPCC official, alleges that while "stabilizing our climate is a huge challenge," the world's "political leaders deserve credit for making this issue a centrepiece of their discussions at the international level." In Collectif Argos's account, global warming constitutes the "last straw" for the impoverished of the world, and not, as seems to be the case, their death sentence. The work, in addition, rather dramatically underestimates the possible number of climate refugees—that is, those who have survived and been displaced by the effects of climate change—as two hundred million by century's end, despite the fact that some twenty million were displaced by unprecedented flooding in Pakistan within a matter of weeks in recent memory. Sadly, the already-horrifying numbers pointed to by the authors regarding the recession of the Himalayan glaciers—that two billion people could be affected by water shortages within fifty to a hundred years—also seem unjustifiably optimistic.[12]

Despite such drawbacks, however, much of the material in *Réfugiés climatiques* is quite good as well as critically important. An Inupiaq woman residing on an island threatened by warming seas in northern Alaska is quoted as saying that she has "trouble imagining a future for [herself]." In Bangladesh, Collectif Argos demonstrates the undeniable dangers posed by rising sea levels, including the penetration of saltwater into bodies of groundwater—a development that quite simply renders agricultural production impossible. Writing honestly, Donatien Garnier, the author of the Bangladesh section, states that the "prospects for survival seem grim." *Réfugiés climatiques* examines the life of Chadians who reside by the ever-retreating shores of Lake Chad and depend on it. As has been mentioned, Lake Chad has undergone a 90 percent reduction in size in the last four decades; Aude Raux, the author of the article on Chad, quotes the United Nations Educational, Scientific, and Cultural Organization as asserting that Lake Chad's fate constitutes "the most spectacular example of the effects of climate change in tropical Africa."[13]

Réfugiés climatiques also explores the phenomenon of the outburst floods of Nepali glacial lakes,
formed through the marked retreat in recent years of the
Himalayan glaciers; these outburst floods undoubtedly
jeopardize the existence of underlying human populations. Raux's article on China at points constitutes a particularly compelling look at migrant labor refugees who,
abandoned by capitalists and government, remind one
of the masses of humanity dispossessed and proletarian-
ized around the world with the introduction of capitalist
social relations. The work's treatment of the expanding
Gobi Desert also illustrates the general trap that capitalism has imposed on Chinese society, as on global society
as a whole: destroying itself environmentally, in addition
to practically enslaving its working class, so as to promote
"development." This dynamic, naturally, has surely been
advanced historically by northern industrial societies before China, as is certainly reflected in the work's sections
on New Orleans, devastated in 2005 by extreme weather,
and on islands threatened by rising sea levels in Germany's
north. But the juxtaposition of the example of northern
China with the threats that warmer oceans pose to the
coral that currently protects the Maldives Islands, or the
disrupted climatic patterns that promote greater rates of
dengue fever on these same islands, serves as commentary
on the pronounced lack of solidarity among southern societies on climate change—a dynamic already experienced
at the 2009 talks in Copenhagen.

In essence, *Réfugiés climatiques* constitutes a stark
warning regarding the "endangered paradise[s]" it

studies—all of them metaphors for the totality of Earth, itself a potential paradise imperiled by climate catastrophe. In its focus on southern peoples and marginalized northerners, the work certainly functions as a reminder of the unmitigated brutality currently being enacted by the contributions of industrial-capitalist societies to climate change as well. Of course, many of the world's regions not discussed in *Réfugiés climatiques* could today be examined similarly, and hopefully in a fruitful fashion; the Sahel, Bolivia and Peru, Mozambique, Russia, and the South Asian subcontinent all come to mind.

The book's value is perhaps best encapsulated in its closing image: Rames Rai, a Nepalese yak-herding boy, is shown running in the mountains with a large grin on his face. It is precisely toward this end—securing the happiness of the world's children, and its peoples as a whole—that radical action must soon be taken to avert the disaster promised by climate change.

Counter-Degradation

The intentional refusal of food products that demand massacre is naturally to be applauded and carried forward, as is the rejection of commodities produced by those who have been effectively enslaved. The mere adoption of individual lifestyle choices, though, clearly fails to prevent the totality of animal slaughter for consumption by humans and nonhuman animals. While it is undeniable that nonhuman animals resist their subjugation by humanity—as is seen in the attacks performed by circus elephants and captive orcas against their trainers—it is obvious that they cannot defend themselves effectively against human violence. Hence, the need for solidarity from among humans themselves.

World Colors

Turtle beaches and whale migrations are manifestations of life that should be cherished rather than destroyed.

Contemplation of the acute failures of human history—the defense of nonhuman life being one central failure—grants ever more reason to the project of "reactivat[ing] the revolutionary fight," as James D. Cockcroft notes on the present-day relevance of the Mexican Revolution.[14] As Adorno writes metaphorically, the mind could not despair over the color gray were it not for its cognizance of different colors altogether.[15]

Toward Home

Approaches that attempt to glean ecological insights from Marx are questionable. As leftist sociologist John Bellamy Foster often stresses, even though Marx expresses concern about the effects of capitalist agriculture on soil nutrient quality and argues that Earth should be handed down to successive generations in a better state than before, there is little sense in Marx that the nonhuman, considered of no instrumental use to humanity, should be valued.[16] Such failures likely follow from Marx's assertion that humanity represents the "sovereign of nature" as well as his call for the "humanization of nature."[17]

These perspectives on nature are not as developed or sympathetic as those of Rosa Luxemburg, who writes of the suffering of a buffalo she encountered as a political prisoner during the First World War: the animal, having been violently exploited for conscription, was then subjected to merciless flogging by its handler. Regarding the animal, Luxemburg observes the "expression on its black face and in its soft black eyes [to be] like that of a weeping child—one that has been severely thrashed and does not know why, nor how to escape from the torment of ill-treatment." When the beast looked at her observing the scene, she writes, "The tears welled from my eyes." She is also pained by the "silent, irresistible extinction" of the "defenseless" warblers whose habitats are decimated by German capitalism. For Luxemburg, concern for the nonhuman should not be separated from a regard for humanity. As she remarks, "I am at home wherever in the world there are clouds, birds and human tears."[18]

Fellow German Marxist Ernst Bloch's vision is similarly compelling: a "socialized humanity" that is "allied" with nature, or "the reconstruction of the world into homeland."[19]

For Novelty

The radical displacement induced by the experience of nature can likewise be communicated in the experience of the negation of beauty. The destruction of rainforests to make way for the raising of cattle, later to be slaughtered, joins the observation of mass collections of refuse in rivers, canyons, and entire oceans as well as the presence in azure shallows of patrol boats, cruise liners, and Jet Skis. This is also found in urban areas, where automobiles, airplanes, police helicopters, and gas-powered lawn mowers, among other things, come into conflict with nature and humanity.

The reduction of the world to private property and advertising space represses orientations sensitive to the vulnerability and fragility of terrestrial life. The system that exterminated many of the indigenous peoples of what is now known as North and South America and relegated many of the descendants of the survivors to reservations has also radically imperiled the biological diversity of life on Earth, beyond having destroyed millions of lives and entire societies outside the Western hemisphere. When people reflect on nature, historical crimes, and possible alternatives, then "consciousness of freedom and anxiety fuse."[20]

Toward Radical Interruption

According to North American environmental activist Bill McKibben, planet Earth has died. Earth's replacement, however, does not constitute progress toward a higher or better state. The newborn planet, named Eaarth by McKibben in his book of the same title, instead develops from the brutality and thoughtlessness engaged in by much of humanity. In McKibben's estimation, the Holocene geological epoch—one that, characterized by a narrow range of fluctuation in average global temperatures, has allowed for humanity's rise and development on Earth over the past twelve thousand years—can no longer be said to exist, due to interference with planetary climate systems as well as human-induced environmental destruction overall.

As an academic concerned with environmental studies, McKibben is aware of the dire nature of the present state of affairs. On the new Eaarth, he mentions that the flow of the Euphrates and Nile rivers could well decline significantly in the near future, and that glacier retreat in the Himalayas and Andes could cause the water supplies of billions of people to dwindle within decades. In light of the various horrors that climate catastrophe could visit on history, McKibben suggests that humanity recognize biophysical limits and jettison "the consumer lifestyle" altogether, instead adopting a "Plan B" characterized by the sharing of resources between northern and southern societies within the context of a joint effort to thoroughly rearrange global society on rational, ecological grounds. Toward the end of attaining an atmospheric carbon concentration of 350 ppm, McKibben endorses what he labels a "clean-tech Apollo mission" and "ecological New Deal," arguing that such thoroughgoing changes be accompanied by a return to small-scale organic agriculture on humanity's part.[21]

Despite the critical perspectives advanced in McKibben's contributions in *Eaarth*, much of the book's argument unfortunately serves present power arrangements, in keeping with McKibben's reformist project. For one, the author blames "modernity," which he defines as "the sudden availability" of "cheap fossil fuel" in the eighteenth century, for the regression to Eaarth and the various possible future scenarios, given climate catastrophe.[22] There is no recognition here, or at any point in the work, of the processes sparked by the onset of the capitalist mode of production during this period of human history; similarly, there is no explicit critique of the highly destructive nature of capitalism in general. It should not be surprising, then, that McKibben's recommendations do not include a call for the abolition of capitalism.

McKibben presents these inadequate reflections while engaging in a tendency to attribute responsibility for the current socioenvironmental predicament to an amorphous "we"—as though the impoverished, the young, and other excluded groups have had any sort of choice on climate policy, let alone the course of history. This line of thought contrasts significantly with views advanced by Chomsky, who in June 2009 suggested the following thought experiment: that North Americans fifty years ago had been given the choice of directing resources toward either the development of "iPods and the internet" or the creation of "a livable and sustainable socioeconomic order"—a false choice, as Chomsky points out, for no such option has ever been on offer.[23] That McKibben claims at one point in *Eaarth* that "we don't pay much attention to poor people" should need little comment, however much this side note says about U.S. liberalism.[24]

Given his recognition of the dire situation today, it is perhaps strange that he does not come to conclusions more substantive than his call for a return to small-scale agriculture coupled with an ominous "green Manhattan project."[25] *Eaarth*, for example, includes little reflection on the terrifyingly repressive actions that capitalists and their defenders may well take to attempt to maintain their privileges within the context of a climate-destabilized world, as examined in Gwynne Dyer's *Climate Wars* (2008). Remarkably, McKibben fails to systematically explore the alarming possible impacts that climate change could have on future agricultural production—considerations that may well prove important for the viability of his "back to the land" project.

McKibben's perspectives are surely far from those advanced by Benjamin. Yet hope for the present predicament may lie in the possibility that contemplation of the profundity of the climate crisis can help move humanity toward adopting Benjamin's concept of revolution—the "attempt by the passengers" on a metaphoric train "to activate the emergency brake" rather than being propelled into the abyss.[26]

Free Nature

For his part, Marcuse sketches a clearer vision of the radically different relationship between humanity and external nature he favors than what can be deduced from Adorno and Horkheimer's *Dialectic of Enlightenment*. Marcuse sees the institution of what he calls a socialist rationality—that is, one "free from [the rationality] of exploitation"—as putting an end to the former experience of self and other as mediated by "aggressive acquisition, competition, and defensive possession."[27] Under these new conditions, external nature would lose "its mere utility," judged not "in terms of its usefulness" or "according to any purpose it may possibly serve," but instead seen as a "life force in its own right."[28] This new, "nonviolent, non-destructive" human-nature relationship, which Marcuse views as a precondition for the self-realization of humanity, is to be characterized by a "letting be" and "acceptance" of the nonhuman other.[29] Where external nature was formerly "mastered and controlled," Marcuse believes it can come to be "liberated" and hence "freely [be] itself."[30]

Love of Life

Politically speaking, James Lovelock's contributions are highly problematic. He states that he believes humanity has not yet evolved to the point at which it could "handle" climate change.[31] Following from this, he urges people to suspend democratic governance, at least temporarily—thereby joining environmental journalist Mark Lynas in calling for a green movement that is "happy with capitalism" and openly promotes the use of nuclear energy.[32] Lovelock's famous Gaia hypothesis may have some explanatory power, and his ongoing advocacy for biodiversity and terrestrial life generally is decidedly important, but his political prescriptions are unpalatable, in addition to being unfounded. Humanity can consciously and anarchically choose to put an end to the social structures as well as ideologies that perpetuate social and environmental devastation. In place of continuing the prevailing catastrophe, it can act differently.

On Hope and Reason Today

What is not can still become.

—Ernst Bloch, *The Principle of Hope*

If the climatological reports synthesized here are remotely accurate—and there seems to be little reason to doubt their integrity, considering the degree to which climatologists' predictions regarding the effects of climate change have been borne out by a number of disastrous occurrences in recent memory—it would seem that humanity's future existence is indeed imperiled. This problematic raises the question of hope today: whether, in Yale anthropologist James C. Scott's words, "the world is heading [our] way."[1]

Initial reflections on this question should emphasize the rather obvious point that the mere existence of hope for social progress—the overthrowing of humanity's oppressors, in Bertolt Brecht's formulation—reflects what Bloch calls the "enduring problem" of the nonrealization of the very conditions sought by hope.[2] Simply put, such conditions are possibilities. As Michael Hardt and Antonio Negri put it, "[If] evil were primary, we would be helpless against it."[3]

Furthermore, Arendt seems entirely correct to claim that the prevention of "evil"—at its most extreme, the "total destruction" that Adorno sees as being the "objective potential" of "bourgeois society"—requires the "exercise of reason as the faculty of thought."[4] Against the twin catastrophes of war and climate destabilization, reason would minimally demand the "preservation of humanity" as a species, in Adorno's words, so as to allow for the possibility of that "self-reflection" that could "transcend" egotistical drives and thus allow humanity to realize revolution.[5] In light of such potentialities, Arendt writes, "thinking itself is dangerous," for it can be employed toward the withdrawal of consent and obedience "to laws, to rulers, to institutions," and a generalized movement to delegitimize a given social regime—one that could under ideal conditions overturn the superior means of violence employed by capital and the state. "This superiority lasts only as long as the power structure of the government is intact—that is, as long as commands are obeyed," observes Arendt. "When this is no longer the case, the situation changes abruptly."[6]

Toward the promotion of abrupt changes in the prevailing state of affairs, this section explores the question of hope and human progress as examined by a selection of thoughtful public intellectuals whose work has contemplated the profound crises of modernity: anarcho-syndicalist Chomsky, critical theorist Adorno, democratic socialist Robert L. Heilbroner, and antiauthoritarian leftist Ronald Aronson.

Chomsky's work is the most contemporary account of the present predicament among the four, although the perspectives advanced by the others are hardly invalidated by their age—a comment on the fact that the "oft-invoked working through of the past has to this day been unsuccessful," that the "causes of what happened" in past catastrophes have failed to date to be "eliminated."[7]

Chomsky: Anarcho-syndicalism qua Progress

For Chomsky, the "primary challenge" faced by the world's peoples today is "decent survival."[8] Human survival, in Chomsky's view, is presently being jeopardized by the specters of war, nuclear annihilation, and environmental collapse. His reflections on these questions dovetail with his concerns regarding evolutionary biologist Ernst Mayr's assertion that the emergence in evolution of the "higher intelligence" afforded humans is little more than a "biological error" that could soon cease to exist, with humans thus joining the billions of other species that have been relegated to extinction since the origins of life.[9] Chomsky shares Mayr's sentiments on the human prospect, for he has variously referred to the present situation as being "the possibly terminal phase of human existence" and, borrowing from Indian journalist Arundhati Roy, the potential "endgame for the human race."[10]

Some of the most serious threats to decent survival are, for Chomsky, those posed by a militarized humanity, especially the increasingly advanced death technologies maintained and developed by dominant power groups. Critical for Chomsky in this sense is consideration of U.S. nuclear weapons policy, which asserts the right to strike first even against nonnuclear states, and recent U.S. efforts to develop tactical nuclear weapons for offensive rather than deterrence use.[11] In addition, U.S. plans to develop ballistic-missile defense programs—begun under George W. Bush and advanced by Barack Obama—are highly disconcerting to Chomsky, for such putatively defensive capabilities could well be used offensively, since they provide their possessors with total defense from retaliatory missile strikes.[12] Because a ballistic missile defense program would be directed from satellite installations in space, such systems are in fact vulnerable to antisatellite attack by means of technologies "readily available" even to those societies Chomsky terms "lesser powers."[13] The furtherance of ballistic missile defense may, then, demand the implementation of a military doctrine of "total spectrum dominance," implying the subjection of terrestrial matters to "overwhelming control" and the advancement of the militarization of space—itself a "major threat to survival."[14] Among other considerations, such policies would likely demand the institution of a "prompt global strike" capability, which would allow its handler (the United States) to attack any target on Earth within a matter of hours or even minutes; it bears mentioning that development of the prompt global strike system has been promoted by the Obama administration, particularly with the August 2011 attempted flight of the Falcon HV-2, a remotely controlled military aircraft that could have traveled at speeds of thirteen thousand miles per hour.[15] Though the test flight

of the Falcon HV-2 thankfully failed, Chomsky is right to
note that the advent of such projects has "no remote historical parallel."[16] They follow from the present organization
of the world, threatened with calamity as it is by the policy
orientations of the United States—a state with historically
unprecedented repressive capacities.

Beyond potentially terminal imperial war, Chomsky
has also identified the severity of the climate predicament
as a threat to survival. Noting the question to be of "tran-
scendent importance," he writes that the environmental crisis "threatens real catastrophe for everyone."[17] "Maybe some
humans will survive" unchecked climate catastrophe, he
remarks, "but it will be scattered and nothing like a decent
existence."[18] Significant changes to avoid such an eventuality are missing in existing society, and Chomsky sees them
as even being inherently at odds with the ruling maxims of
the given order. In capitalism, he asserts, short-term profits
outweigh long-term considerations, and externalities—the
"side effects" or "collateral damage" of profit-seeking behavior—must be ignored for normal production to exist, even
if, as in the case of climate change, "the externalities happen
to be the fate of the species."[19] Chomsky also believes that
responsibility for the climate crisis lies in the tendency to
dismiss the interests of those who, possessing little to no
economic resources, are considered in the ill-named democracy of the market to have no interests at all, particularly the materially impoverished as well as future generations.
It follows, he writes, that those who accept this institutional assemblage will work to "destroy the possibility for
decent survival for our grandchildren, if by so doing [they]

can maximize [their] own 'wealth.'"[20] Within existing arrangements, then, "profits for the next quarter (leading to huge bonuses for the CEOs)" are valued more than continued human existence.[21] The "dedicated efforts" that have been taken to dismantle institutions designed to "mitigate the harsh consequences of market fundamentalism" are principally to blame in this sense, along with those efforts launched against the "culture of sympathy and solidarity."[22]

The threats that Chomsky identifies to the prospect of decent human survival are formidable. Despite the grave implications of having existing technologies be largely controlled by capitalists and state managers—agents who respond to little other than profit and power—Chomsky nonetheless stresses that the present predicament should not be considered a historical aberration. The unprecedented present "near-monopoly of the means of large-scale violence in the hands of one state"—the United States—can be said to follow from the conquest of "most of the world" by Europe and its settler societies—a process greatly accelerated by the events of 1492, and subsequently carried forward by the "development" trajectory implied by colonial-capitalist control of vast foreign territories and labor forces.[23] The Allied victory in World War II left the United States as the reigning superpower, and the collapse of the Soviet Union only strengthened the U.S. position as world ruler. Though it should be uncontroversial to observe that those with power and privilege act to protect and defend such power and privilege, an understanding of this dynamic can greatly help to explain the prevailing situation. In this sense, Chomsky's drawing of parallels between the actions of the United States since its rise to superpower status in the mid-twentieth century and the efforts of the reactionary Austrian Count Metternich and Russian czars to hold then-prevailing power relations is instructive.[24] It helps account for a particularly salient characteristic of global political experience as subordinated to U.S. power: the fierce repression by the United States and its various allies of what Oxfam has termed the "threat of a good example," or "successful independent development," as in Cuba, Guatemala, Nicaragua, and Vietnam, to name only a handful of rebellious societies that have met with the U.S. "Mafia" doctrine: that disobedience, a "virus" that "spread[s] contagion," cannot be tolerated—that "the idea of taking matters into [one's] own hands" must be repressed.[25] "The threat," as Caribbean scholar Nick Nesbitt notes, "is one of ideological contamination."[26] It is reproduced, for one, in the alternative that highland stateless societies represent to the captive subjects of Southeast Asian *padi* states, and in those alternatives posed to centralized power by the Parisian sections of the French Revolution of 1789 and the soviets after 1917.[27]

The United States can hardly be said to have a monopoly on the practice of Chomsky's Mafia doctrine, in light of similar actions taken by powerful states from Israel to the Russian Federation. The doctrine is a practice following from the existence of hierarchical power structures in the first place and the violent efforts taken by those privileged by such arrangements to maintain such power relations. Perhaps most important, though, an understanding of this dynamic may go some way in explaining the marked absence today of substantive spaces dedicated to the advancement of social revolution.

Though the correlation of present-day forces is undoubtedly dire, Chomsky, as an Enlightenment rationalist, holds this reality to be socially contingent. The policy choices that enhance the threats to survival posed by militarism and environmental catastrophe are formulated by elite classes the world over—individuals whom Chomsky refers to as the "principal architects of policy"—themselves constrained by their embeddedness within prevailing institutional frameworks championing capitalist profit along with the maintenance and furtherance of domination as fundamental ends to be advanced.[28] If these two aspects of global society can somehow be overcome, Chomsky argues, rationality and humanity may in fact be allowed to prevail, and the various threats to human survival be resolved.

Critical for the project of avoiding "severe consequences for the species" is in Chomsky's view a radical reconsideration of the "sectors that are in a position to determine policy."[29] In the U.S. context, Chomsky identifies this agent as being the presently dormant "second superpower," or the general public, which under normal conditions is relegated to being little more than a spectator observing the work of "responsible" functionaries of capital and the state.[30] Mirroring recommendations made by Jacques Rancière for the "part that has no part" to intervene in the political world, Chomsky calls for an "aroused public" to engage in popular mobilizations that seek to disrupt hegemonic politics and remake society along lines radically different than those propagated by dominant interests to date.[31] In concrete terms, he writes of the "authentic hope" to be gleaned from the grassroots campaigning efforts that propelled Obama to the presidency—that is, that those who have been "organized to take instructions from the leader might 'break free,'" and come to participate directly in the deliberation on and formulation of policymaking, which is usually considered to be the reserve of the political class.[32] The various atrocities engaged in by the United States and its allies—as well as those advanced by power structures independent of U.S. influence and power projection—can in Chomsky's view only be halted if "inhibited from within," for only the subjects of rights-violating states can enforce the demands stipulated by international law, to say nothing of reason.[33] The employment of "scrutiny" against "concentrated power" is instrumental toward this end—a responsibility that in Chomsky's mind goes together with the obligation to "enter the moral arena in a serious way" by means of "help[ing] suffering people as best we can."[34]

Though Chomsky repeatedly stresses that progress toward such realities demands radical action above all in the United States, the core of the global system—and in this sense echoes the conclusions of German psychologist Wilhelm Reich, who stresses that "masses of working men [sic] will not be relieved of their social responsibility" but rather "*burdened* with it," along with those of many autonomous Marxist theorists, who find the problem of capitalism to be not the imposition of capital on to workers but instead the complicity of workers themselves in perpetuating capitalism—the contributions of an "informed and engaged public, worldwide" are hardly unimportant in Chomsky's calculus.[35] In particular, Chomsky's continued endorsement of anarchism—what he calls the institution of "truly democratic societies" that "overtur[n] structures of hierarchy and domination," and are "based on popular control of social, economic, political, and cultural institutions"—should be read as advocacy of a political project for the world instead of only isolated communities.[36] All "students" should become anarchists, declares Chomsky, just as there should be "democratic control of every institution."[37]

Were the normally excluded masses to come to replace the existing overseers as policymakers, rational alternatives to the threats of war and climate change could indeed be considered viable options. One means to this end emphasized by Chomsky is the establishment of a nuclear weapons free zone or even a weapons of mass destruction free zone in southwestern Asia, given that such a move could significantly ease tensions between the United States/Israel and Iran regarding the question of the latter's nuclear weapons capabilities.[38] As the possibility of armed conflict passing beyond the nuclear threshold is perhaps highest at present in the Middle East, it follows that priority should be placed on establishing such zones there first, although this should not be taken to mean that other regions of the world could not be similarly explosive: one thinks of India and Pakistan, for example. Given that even a nuclear conflict constrained to a relatively small region of the globe could well provoke a nuclear winter that would prove catastrophic to peoples unaffected by the direct impact of a nuclear weapons exchange and its fallout, as reviewed in recent memory by Fidel Castro, it follows that the world as a whole should itself become a nuclear weapon or weapons of mass destruction free zone.[39] As with wildlife reserves, whether marine or land based, merely declaring certain regions of Earth free from such weapons would however do little to protect the world from noncooperating states and regions. Thankfully, support for disarmament policies has apparently been reported among large majorities of the U.S. and Iranian publics—hence Chomsky's conclusion that "functioning democracy might alleviate severe dangers" to decent human survival.[40] Were such publics to come to power, the massive resources dedicated to the military could be redirected to more productive ends.

Beyond providing alternatives to militarization and war, Chomsky's conception of democratic societies could also offer much-needed policy regarding climate change. Liberated from the strictures of capitalism, global society could "move with dispatch toward conservation and renewable energy," and in particular dedicate "substantial resources" toward "harnessing solar energy," though in Chomsky's view human society would necessarily have to overturn the "huge state-corporate social engineering projects of the post–World War II period" based on "wasteful reliance on fossil fuels" while also "dismantl[ing]" the "entire sociological, cultural, economic, and ideological structure which is just driving [humankind] to disaster."[41] In particular, Chomsky sees great promise in the prospect of redesigning the U.S. manufacturing base so as to advance the project of mitigating climate change, as is commensurate with his anarcho-syndicalism: "One of the things that could happen is that the workers in [General Motors] plants could simply take over the factories and say, Okay, we're going to construct and develop, we're going to reconvert, we're going to develop high-speed rail, which they have the capacity to do."[42]

Catastrophe and Redemption in Adorno's Work

The contemplation of catastrophe and historical regression were primary questions for Adorno. He asked "whether culture, and whatever culture has become, permits something like the good life," whether the "good life" is possible "within the bad one," whether the "right form of politics" lies "within the realm of what can be achieved today," and "whether humankind is able to prevent catastrophe."[43]

For Adorno, speaking after the military defeat of Nazism, "any appeal to the idea of progress would seem absurd given the scale of the catastrophe [of the industrial genocide perpetrated by the Nazi regime]."[44] The "totality" in which Adorno finds himself is for him "odious and abhorrent," as it reduces people to the "level of objects," thus "radically erod[ing]" the "possibility of the good life."[45] The prevailing *Weltlauf*, or course of the world, "continues to hold a pistol to the heads of human beings," and the "dream that humanity would organize the world humanely" is one that "the actual world of humanity is resolutely eradicating."[46] In messianic terms, Adorno claims that the "name of history may not be spoken," as "what would truly be history, the other, has not yet begun."[47] In his view, the very chance for freedom has "sunk to such a minimal level" that it calls into question the possibility of moral action in the world. At the very least, he says, the nature of existing society would "necessarily lead almost everyone to protest."[48] Though it is unclear whether this call in particular should be taken as equivalent to the Russian "Все на баррикады!" ("Everyone to the barricades!"), at other points Adorno finds space for antisystemic violence.[49]

The present, Adorno argues, could give birth to "both utopian and absolutely destructive possibilities."[50] In conversation with his colleague Horkheimer, he claims that "we should talk to mankind [sic] once again as in the eighteenth century: you are upholding a system that threatens to destroy you."[51] In light of such considerations, nothing less than the "prevention and avoidance of total catastrophe" constitutes for Adorno "the possibility of progress," for only if catastrophe were averted could progress be said to exist.[52] In Adorno's view, progress is indelibly linked to "the survival of the species." There can be no progress without the realization of the "happiness of unborn generations"—an idea Adorno takes from the work of his comrade Benjamin as constituting the very "notion of redemption."[53] Progress, moreover, can exist only if humanity "as a whole can be said to progress," for progress only in some areas is for Adorno no progress at all.[54] This position—itself close to Bakunin's claim that freedom exists only under conditions in which "all human beings, men and women, are equally free"—is reiterated elsewhere when Adorno asserts that there is "no emancipation without that of society."[55] Adorno's account of progress here can also be compared fruitfully with that of French socialist and feminist Simone de Beauvoir, who holds that "the existence of others" in "freedom" is the very "condition of [one's] own freedom."[56] For Adorno, indeed, the prospect of progress presupposes the as yet unfulfilled historical possibility for the "establishment of humankind," since insofar as "humankind remains entrapped by the totality which it itself fashions," he writes, "progress has not yet taken place at all."[57]

Prevailing reality thus allows for the possibility of total regression, but the chance to both avoid and abolish such a threat is in Adorno's view "still not without all hope," as he "believe[s] that things can come right in the end."[58] Adorno contends in Hegelian terms that "part of the dialectic of progress is that historical setbacks ... provide the condition needed for humanity to find the means to avert them in the future."[59] Like Benjamin, who sees in "every second" of the future "the door through which the Messiah could enter," Adorno suggests that progress can begin "at any instant."[60] Adorno contrasts his own position in this sense from that of Hegel and Marx, with the former finding the realization of reason in the historical emergence of the state, and the latter maintaining that communism is born out of capitalism, instead stating that freedom "has been possible at every moment."[61]

Expressing claims similar to those made by Chomsky and anarchist social theorist Murray Bookchin, among others, Adorno argues that the already-existing "material base" provided by the historical trajectory taken by the capitalist mode of production—and specifically, its technologies—could be redirected and reorganized to supply a reasonable life for all humans.[62] Asserting in rationalist terms that "the responsibility for the threats that the advancing sciences unleash on [humanity]" is to be found "not with reason or science" but rather in the manner in which "reason is *entwined* with very real social relations," Adorno claims that "no one on earth needs to suffer poverty," because the state of productive forces could in theory "free the world from want."[63] "For the first time," even "violence might vanish altogether."[64] The promising potentialities Adorno sees in technology, for instance, are expressed in a rare deviation from his notorious reluctance to positively sketch out social redemption when he mentions that societies could be organized "far more rationally" in small, decentralized units from which "all those aggressive and destructive tendencies would have been banished," and that could thus "collaborate peaceably with one another."[65]

The "philosophy of reflection" is central to the prospect of realizing the "utopian possibilities" that Adorno envisages.[66] Such a philosophy would develop out of the promise of a "critical confrontation with society as it actually exists"—one that would result in the overhaul of existing reality toward ends other than prevailing ones.[67]

Adorno sees such critical thought by itself, though, as insufficient, for "reason's helpful self-reflection . . . would be its transition to praxis." He agrees here with his comrade Horkheimer, who claims theory to be "authentic" only "where it serves practice."[68] Adorno and Horkheimer's emphasis on the need for such action aimed at rearranging social relations should not be underestimated: human survival itself is in jeopardy, Adorno states, if a "self-conscious global subject does not develop and intervene." The very "possibility of progress," then, "has devolved to this subject alone."[69] In this sense, the "awakening" of humanity is "the sole potential for a coming of age," and progress is to be attained through a "coming out of the spell." It is only when "humanity becomes aware of its own indigenousness to nature and brings to a halt the domination it exacts over nature through which domination by nature continues" that progress can exist, according to Adorno. The domination of humanity and of nature must be halted, writes Adorno; paradoxically, "progress occurs only where it ends."[70]

As exhilarating as Adorno's account of the prospect of humanity's awakening may be, Adorno himself seems to have long been pessimistic about the possibility of its actual realization. In "Progress," he quite plainly observes that "the idea of a progress which leads out and away is presently blocked . . . because the subjective moments of spontaneity are beginning to wither in the historical process."[71] Adorno's view here is doubtlessly informed by what he and Horkheimer refer to as the "culture industry" in *Dialectic of Enlightenment*: the socialization processes of existing society that work to "ensure that the simple reproduction of mind does not lead on to the expansion of mind" through formal education, the mass media, television, and the dominant culture. In these theorists' disturbing account, such processes reign within the existing society, creating a "totally administered world" and hence fettering humanity in large part to the "gigantic apparatus."[72]

As serious as Adorno and Horkheimer considered the threat of the culture industry to freedom and historical progress, the former seems not necessarily to have believed that the colonization of mind propagated by existing social relations implies the absolute victory of capitalism and other authoritarian social relations. "No light falls on [humans] and things without reflecting transcendence," Adorno writes toward the end of *Negative Dialectics*. "All happiness is but a fragment of the entire happiness men [*sic*] are denied."[73] Though the mindlessness promoted by the culture industry is to a degree generally accepted by people, it is at times done so with "a kind of reservation," Adorno contends, and it is perhaps even "not quite believed in."[74] This principle is well reflected in a 1955 study Adorno authored examining group attitudes among Germans about the Second World War and the experience of National Socialism; the close of the study considers those individuals who expressed reasonable and humane perspectives opposed to war, militarism, and racism.[75] Adorno's fundamental position is best described in his following comments to Horkheimer: "On the one hand, the world contains opportunities enough for success. On the other hand, everything is bewitched, as if under a spell. If the spell could be broken, success would be a possibility."[76]

Even Horkheimer, perhaps the more resigned of these two theorists, expresses similar faith in humanity's potential: "Mutilated as men [*sic*] are, in the duration of a brief moment they can become aware that in the world which has been thoroughly rationalized they can dispense with the interests of self-preservation which still set them one against the other."[77]

Once the uninhibited interest of self-preservation itself is transcended, humans then can transcend "destruction," violence, and the "megaton bomb."[78] Reason then can be employed, as Horkheimer writes, to "recognize and denounce the forms of injustice and thus emancipate itself from them."[79] Hence the importance Adorno reserves for the practice of reason, since in his view only reason alone is capable of abolishing domination—hence and also his hypothetical assertion that "finally progress can begin, at any instant."[80]

Heilbroner: To Be Atlas

Also worthy of consideration for the present crisis are Heilbroner's reflections in *An Inquiry into the Human Prospect*—a work that attempts to answer the question of whether there is hope for humanity.[81]

Heilbroner begins by asking whether the likely future of humanity can be imagined as something other than a perpetuation of the "darkness, cruelty, and disorder of the past," and especially whether a "catastrophe of fearful proportions" is looming. His answer—after considering the problems of human population, warfare, ecological devastation, and technological development—is quite simply that there is no reason for hope. Against the resignation that could follow from such a conclusion, though, he comes to moderate this claim by clarifying that he does not hold the

human prospect to be "an irrevocable death sentence" or
that humanity is headed toward an "inevitable doomsday"
but rather that "the risk of enormous catastrophe exist[s],"
and that these serious obstacles must be overcome before
human survival can be assured. These challenges can be
resolved by the intervention of human mindfulness, says
Heilbroner, though he stresses that nature, too, could similarly resolve such problems by means of the collapse of the
ecological conditions that underpin human society.

For Heilbroner, contemplation on the human prospect
necessitates an examination of the "dangers of the know-
able external challenges of the future" as well as an evalu-
ation of humanity's ability to meet such challenges. He
imagines that the future will bring with it resource wars,
whereby impoverished southern societies develop nuclear
weapons so as to force northern societies into engaging in
mass-redistribution schemes. Heilbroner does not expect
future violence to consist exclusively of such South-on-
North conflict, for continued aggression by rich nations
against poor will surely complement it.[82] He mentions
the possibility that industrialized societies will embark
on "wars of 'preemptive seizure'" to secure access to critical natural resources, even and especially those located in
the Global South. Rather strangely, however, and in sharp
contrast to many contemporary commentators, Heilbroner
exerts little energy pondering the threat of nuclear war
and concomitant human annihilation. Yet he does suggest that a voluntary redistribution of wealth from North
to South could help avoid the large-scale human suffering
he sees as likely, in light of population growth patterns and

impending ecological decline—although only if such re-distribution schemes are promoted on a large enough scale. Reviewing the number of interstate conflicts in the decades since the 1940s, Heilbroner somewhat helpfully concludes that such wars can be expected to continue as long as states exist, though he foresees no exit from this situation.[83]

Another critical challenge Heilbroner sees for the human prospect is the environmental consequences following from the adoption of industrial technology. Even if nuclear attacks are somehow avoided, Heilbroner asserts that human society is rapidly approaching the end point of Earth's systems to support "industrial activity," thus allying himself with the Club of Rome and other contemporary socioenvironmental observers. Anticipating that which eco-Marxist James O'Connor terms the second contradiction of capitalism, Heilbroner maintains that a grave decline in material living conditions might result from modernity's "massive assault against the biosphere." In particular, he identifies the threat of "serious climatic problems" due to the ever-increasing surplus heat emission produced by industrial processes and argues that this may be the most formidable challenge faced by humanity. He asserts, rather optimistically, that the climate threat is a distant one—hence his claim that the climatic limits to industrial activity will become evident within three or four generations, after which "industrial growth" will have to be completely halted, for its continuation beyond this point in time would, on Heilbroner's account, ensure extinction. He nonetheless prefers that growth be put to an end some time before this point is reached, advocating the widespread adoption of solar energy and other renewable energy sources. For Heilbroner, the environmental crisis as a whole—the prospect of climate catastrophe, but also the various other ecological problems induced by modernity—demands that industrial activity be "drastically curtailed" or even dismantled.[84]

The problem of science and technology is, in Heilbroner's view, connected to the environmental crisis. The development of science has overemphasized "disequilibrating or perilous aspects without giving rise to enough benign technologies or compensating control measures." Claiming that science and technology are the principal forces of the age, Heilbroner bases the contemporary predicament in "the advent of a command over natural processes and forces that far exceeds the reach of our present mechanisms of social control"—reification, in the terminology of Western Marxists. It follows from this that the horrors toward which modernity is propelling humanity do not come out of nowhere, for they are caused by humans, and thus can be changed by humans. In this sense, Heilbroner argues that the prevailing frameworks in which much of this human behavior takes place—industrial civilization, as he calls it—are the main problem. The "socialism" practiced in the Soviet Union is insufficiently different from capitalism to merit endorsement from Heilbroner as an alternative, in light of its endorsement of efficiency, productivism, increased material consumption, and the domination of nature.[85]

Heilbroner does hold out the possibility that under different conditions, matters could be made radically

different too. He offers the example of a polity characterized by "extensive decentralization," "workers' control,"
and "an atmosphere of political and social freedom," but
does not dwell on this alternative—instead embarking
on a discussion of whether capitalism could bring about
a stationary state, as advocated by John Stuart Mill and
Herman Daly, among others. Heilbroner naturally observes that no capitalist society has yet to seriously consider the scale of change needed to achieve something
approximating a viable steady state. Nonetheless, he ac-
knowledges that many of the thoroughgoing changes in
social relations that would need to be realized if global
society were to stave off catastrophe—the "control over
the direction of science, over its rate of incorporation in
technology, and over the pace of industrial production as
a whole"—would more easily be effected under conditions from which considerations of capitalist profit have
been eradicated.[86]

Though Heilbroner devotes relatively little of his
Inquiry to reconstructive political projects, he lays out
some of the basic features of the path he feels would lead
away from the prevailing state of affairs. For one, impoverished southern societies could come to redefine the term
development through stressing the "education and vital-
ity of their citizens" over the quest for capital accumulation. Major efforts in northern societies to minimize the
"enormous wastefulness of industrial production as it is
used today" could contribute to the success of this project.
Heilbroner also holds out the prospect of a reduction in
scale from "immense nation-states" to human communities

emulating the polis of the ancient Greeks, and suggests that simplicity and frugality must come to replace prevailing consumerism. For Heilbroner, the chance that these alternative institutions could emerge and sustain themselves remains possible, though rather improbable, as he sees an undeniable need for a centralization of political power to carry through the myriad social transformations that are in his view required to uphold the human prospect, especially given his pessimism regarding the question of whether people will consent to proposed socioeconomic overhauls. Heilbroner emphatically proclaims that "no substantial voluntary diminution of growth, much less a planned reorganization of society, is today even remotely imaginable." Beyond structural considerations, Heilbroner claims that this is largely the case because of the radically limited capacity he sees for humans to empathize and identify with peoples of other societies as well as future generations—such empathy and identification being, in Heilbroner's account, a necessary prerequisite of popular advocacy of the social changes he endorses.[87]

On the specific question of whether existing generations can be said to possess a "collective bond of identity" to future generations, Heilbroner desperately extrapolates from what he defines as prevailing attitudes:

> When men [*sic*] can generally acquiesce in, even relish, the destruction of their living contemporaries, when they can regard with indifference or irritation the fate of those who live in slums, rot in prison, or starve in lands that have meaning

only insofar as they are vacation resorts, why should they be expected to take the painful actions needed to prevent the destruction of future generations whose faces they will never see?[88]

Such an indictment, perhaps Heilbroner's most fundamentally challenging observation, is reminiscent of similar comments made by Horkheimer: "The human species which devours other animal species, the nations with bursting granaries that allow others to starve, the decent folk who live next door to the prisons where the poor vegetate in stench and misery because they wanted a better life or could not stand it any longer—they are all criminal if crime means an objective abomination."[89]

In the end, suggests Heilbroner, little more is left than disjointed attempts to "preserve the very will to live." Heilbroner allows for the possibility that a "survivalist ethic" may somehow emerge among specific groups of human communities; the stark alternative is for global human polities to be reduced to "the executioners of [humanity]."[90]

Aronson's Collective Action against Madness

Writing over twenty-five years ago, Aronson considers much the same question in his *Dialectics of Disaster: A Preface to Hope* as that driving Heilbroner's *Inquiry*: is there reason for hope? Aronson begins his exploration by citing Gil Elliot in his claim that the "scale of man-made death is the central moral as well as material fact of our time"—this, in the closing years of the twentieth century, a time period that has constituted a "charnel house" in which "revolutionary expectations have been so thwarted."[91]

Examining some of the various lapses of that century—the Nazi genocide of European Jewry, the "Soviet Holocaust" prosecuted by Leninism and Stalinism after 1917, the "bourgeois-democratic holocaust" of the Vietnam War, the dispossession and oppression visited on the Palestinian people by Zionism, and the possibility of a "universal holocaust" by means of nuclear annihilation—Aronson reaches several conclusions about the reasons for the emergence of such social disasters. One fundamental commonality is the complicity of social majorities with prevailing reality—the often-remarkable lack of popular resistance to inhuman sociopolitical projects. Echoing some of Arendt's commentary on the experience of Nazi and Soviet totalitarianisms at points, Aronson stresses the importance that repressive ideologies—nationalism, racism, and corrupted senses of Hegelianism—have had in legitimizing decidedly illegitimate practices. Distancing himself from accounts of genocide that find static national cultures responsible for such crimes, Aronson argues that "no form of society is exempt from becoming genocidal," noting that "*any* contemporary ruling class or national group is capable of using the modern state's weapons for catastrophic purposes." Citing U.S. psychologist Stanley Milgram's investigations into authority, Aronson contends that the tendency to obey within hierarchical apparatus helps explain the Nazi experience, but he also stresses the active complicity of many and the "silent acquiescence" of others as important considerations. Stalinism, Aronson finds, developed directly out of the October 1917 Bolshevik takeover, and the genocide perpetrated during the Vietnam War was prosecuted by a "smoothly functioning society at the peak of its wealth and power."[92]

Writing of the contemporary world, Aronson notes the limited resistance to "increasingly mad mainstreams," lamenting madness as being "ascendant over the oppositional forces of sanity and humanity it continues to generate." With nuclear weapons in mind, Aronson writes that "human life itself has been put in question by the people and technology who ostensibly serve it," making the following crucial point: "To jeopardize life on any scale without compelling reason, and to do this while denying that one is doing it, is mad." Against this, Aronson holds out the promise of an antiauthoritarian classless society in which "ordinary people really do exercise collective control over their lives." He claims humanity's inability to institute such a set of social relations as being at the very root of the threat of nuclear annihilation.[93]

Similar to Arendt and Adorno, Aronson concludes that the social catastrophes he explores need not occur again, if enough people thoughtfully reflect on historical terror and engage in action that seeks to prevent its reoccurrence. Claiming "evil" to "always [be] a human project," he declares that its practice therefore is not necessarily a given. He believes that people will struggle for reason and justice as long as the human species exists. Aronson thus finds hope in the prospect of collective human action aimed at "*bring[ing] about* survival, peace, and well-being," at instituting a better world that will "respect both its source and its ultimate term (people), and will abolish the conditions that led to Auschwitz, the Gulag, Vietnam." Political action is for Aronson the only possible means of resolving societal madness, since "the commitment to sanity, to truth, to humanity, to survival, means doing battle." Considering in particular the universal holocaust threatened by nuclear weapons, Aronson hopes that humanity will "awaken from [its] delusions, as the Nazis never did, to attack the social structures responsible for the impending disaster."[94]

Toward a Critical Appraisal

What, then, can be made of this? A fair bit, in fact. Much in the perspectives advanced by these four authors, as that of other serious theorists, is critical in light of the present predicament.

The desperate urgency of the accounts presented should not be taken as exaggerated or unfounded, for the fact of the matter is that the very survival of humanity is imperiled, as these authors claim. It is rather unclear how one should act in the face of what Castro terms this "terribly sad reality" (*tristísima realidad*).[95] For the victims of climate change, past and present, there is no hope—only despair. Any account of the issue of global warming that does not make this concern central is radically false.

The disorientation accompanying the recognition that the current situation jeopardizes the future reproduction of human society is certainly alarming. Reflection on the problem could promote wild confusion, as Heilbroner notes, for it challenges the very standing of legitimate action in the world. Certainly one concern is the possibility that people in general, once having come to reflect on the radically absurd nature of the prevailing state of affairs, will conclude that the situation is hopeless, and subsequently further retreat from engaging with the public sphere and political matters, thereby perpetuating existing arrangements.[96] Heilbroner raises this worry, which in turn McKibben has also recently done.[97] Yet Heilbroner himself has little patience for such a position. Echoing Camus, he writes that "avoidable evil remains, as it always will, an enemy that can be defeated; and the fact that the collective destiny of man [sic] portends unavoidable travail is no reason, and cannot be tolerated as an excuse, for doing nothing."[98]

One of the most important contributions made by these authors is the stress they place on the fact that however catastrophic the designs of constituted power, humanity's "global societal constitution" is contingent; it can be changed, as it is the result of given political and cultural institutions, social and economic structures, and ideologies. Such a critical position is the very foundation for hope today.[99] Revolutionary humanist commitment and action are not traits that are foreign to humanity, as Chomsky rightly notes; where they are present, they can be carried forward, and where they are missing, they can be revitalized.[100] All the authors examined in this section, except for the ambiguous Heilbroner, hold such faith in humanity's potentialities. The confidence that Chomsky, Adorno, and Aronson hold for the chance to overcome catastrophe and establish something approximating reason seems far more convincing than Heilbroner's pessimism.

Another significant aspect of these authors' accounts—itself inseparable from claims about the contingency of prevailing society—is their anticapitalist perspective. Heilbroner, for one, is certainly justified in questioning economic growth on environmental grounds, as such environmental commentators as George Monbiot, James Gustav Speth, and John Bellamy Foster, among others, have also done. For his part, Chomsky holds the capitalist mode of production directly responsible for looming environmental catastrophe, while Aronson sees it as a key component of the general societal madness that threatens the human prospect. Capitalism, in Adorno's view, is part and parcel of the monstrous apparatus that perpetuates radical human alienation. In his call for humanity's "debarbarization," Adorno would likely agree with Cornelius Castoriadis's claim that "the present cris[e]s of humanity will be able to be resolved only through a socialist revolution."[101]

Nonetheless, Heilbroner's critique of "industrial activity"—a position that seems not terribly far from that of primitivism—seems fairly mistaken. His concerns regarding the environmental destructiveness of economic expansion as practiced under both Western capitalism and Soviet-style state capitalism are justified, for both systems have been thoroughly discredited on these grounds, as on many others. His mistake nonetheless begins in seeing these two regimes as the only alternatives open to humanity. If a society used industrial production to produce essential

medicines or energy from solar or wind power, for example, it would not necessarily be unsustainable. The more
relevant consideration here regards the nature of social
relations, particularly economic ones.

As the three other theorists argue, a reorganization of
existing technologies on a basis different than that dictated
by growth economies, whether capitalist or Soviet, together
with efforts dedicated to further technological innovation
aimed at drastically reducing human suffering as well as min-
imizing or even reversing human destruction of the nonhuman world, would be instrumental in improving humanity's
prospects. Rationality and humanity demand that humans
dedicate themselves, as Horkheimer asserts, to assisting
people, caring for the sick, and aiding the poor, in place of
valorizing capital and perpetuating the prevailing modes of
domination, including especially those that maintain alienated labor and warfare.[102] In light of the climate predicament,
moreover, these demands should definitively include calling
for a radical reduction in greenhouse gas emissions within
the near future. This, in turn, necessitates what Adorno calls
a "global self-conscious subject" or Chomsky dubs a "second
superpower," armed with a recognition of Neumann's claim
that "the primary fact of modern civilization is this very an-
tagonism between an economy that can produce in abun-
dance for welfare but that does so only for destruction."[103]
Autonomous action exercised by the subordinated could
model itself after the historical experience of the 1871 Paris
Commune, the workers' councils that arose in the general
strike wave that gripped Russia in 1905, the soviet-based
democracy that briefly flourished in Russia in the wake of

czardom's collapse, anarchist upheaval in Catalunya in the 1930s, worker and student mobilizations in May 1968, and indeed the various oppositional developments that emerged in 2011—in addition to the speculative reflections of Ursula K. Le Guin's *The Dispossessed*, Ernest Callenbach's *Ecotopia*, and Kim Stanley Robinson's Mars trilogy (*Red Mars*, *Green Mars*, and *Blue Mars*).

To assess the chance of a revolutionary interruption of society's prevailing direction, it is crucial to first take account of the various threats to decent survival. The gravity of the climate crisis has already been discussed here, but it's worth restating the urgency of the situation—to declare, with Horkheimer, that humanity is destroying itself.[104] Beyond the barbarism promised by climate destabilization, militarism and the specter of military conflict in the foreseeable future threaten humanity. The much-celebrated election of Obama as U.S. president has seen the marked continuation of previously existing barbarism. His administration has requested "defense" budgets larger than those overseen by Bush at the end of his time in power and has advanced the development of a number of alarming weapons-system programs—the principal ones in this sense being thirteen-ton "massive ordnance penetrators" designed to be dropped on deeply buried bunkers from B-52 bombers, arms found by Chomsky to be "the most lethal weapons in the [U.S] arsenal short of nuclear weapons"; the prompt global strike system and Falcon HV-2; and the X-37B and X-47B, unstaffed machines to be launched into space for surveillance purposes and, it is to be imagined, possible space-to-Earth strikes.[105] Current near-term plans to utilize agrofuel sources as part of U.S. military operations are similarly worrying, given the well-known conflict between agrofuel and food cultivation—and this under conditions in which some one billion individuals are undernourished, with billions more expected to starve because of climate change.[106] The sixty billion dollar sale of U.S. arms to Saudi Arabia in 2010, war preparations against Iran, and Obama's drone war over Pakistan, which has killed hundreds of Pakistani noncombatants, all offer glimpses of what can be expected from continuing to employ such disconcerting technologies—illustrations of the wrongly developed nature of a false society, on Horkheimer's account.[107] For their part, the millions murdered and displaced in the aftermath of the U.S. invasion of Iraq would demand that nothing similar recur in the future.

Such a brief account of some of the more frightening implications of militarism today necessarily stresses the central role of the United States in the perpetuation of contemporary problems, but this should in no way be taken to mean that other existing regimes have overturned the maxims that govern dominant groups in the United States—for one would be hard-pressed to find other states that are significantly opposed to these approaches. This fact has much to do with the realities of U.S. hegemony, yet this critique should not overlook hegemony exercised elsewhere—such as Han Chinese over Tibetans, Brahmins over Dalits, men of all places over women and children, and heterosexuals over nonheterosexuals. The presupposition of universal human equality should manifest itself as a universal opposition to oppression.

The central question is whether humanity, or at least a significant part of it, is preparing for a critical confrontation with prevailing power structures. Given the gravity of the present crisis, everything depends on this. Social resistance can be found among several existing political movements, and opposition to the prevailing state of affairs can be observed in much of everyday life, as explored by Bloch and John Holloway, among others.[108] The far more obvious reality, however, is that the world is radically wrong, and that no existing force seems capable of overturning the present state of affairs. "Too little that is good has power in the world for the world to be said to have achieved progress," in Adorno's words, just as "there is [presently] no resolute and sufficiently unified anti-capitalist movement that can adequately challenge the reproduction of the capitalist class and the perpetuation of its power on the world stage," as Harvey concludes.[109]

While Adorno's diagnosis of political apathy as "the universal rule in all countries now" was surely mistaken in 1964, just as it is in 2012, popular alienation is still strong in the present global system.[110] Indeed, this remarkable lack of democracy (power of the people, as in the Greek *demos* + *kratia*) seems to be a trend far more present than any opposing countercurrent, notwithstanding the dramatic impulses expressed in the recent popular Arab rebellions and occupy/decolonize movements. Even though Castoriadis's assertion that "the peoples of the world are complicit with the world-course" is an unfair exaggeration, it is true that many individuals and groups of people—say, particularly the middle classes of industrialized northern

societies—identify with as well as actively support the
monstrousness of the present. Heilbroner's reservations
about the egotistical, aggressive character structure en-
couraged by the reign of capital, themselves reflections of
concerns expressed by critical psychoanalyst Erich Fromm
throughout his life, seem well founded. Arendt, for one,
is right to stress that one reason why "totalitarian regimes
can get so far" is that people generally indulge in "wishful
thinking" and "shir[k] reality in the face of real insanity"
rather than rebelling.[111] The phenomenon of societal mi-
mesis—the chameleonlike tendency to adjust to and accept
given reality—is tied into this dynamic, because generalized conformity tends to induce what U.S. antimilitarist
philosopher Henry Giroux terms a "moral coma."[112] That
everyone en masse should be manifesting a clear opposition
to the status quo is a demand more pressing now than in
any previous era. The lack of conscious opposition among
those relatively privileged in material and political terms
speaks to the degree that many northern residents have
been colonized and integrated into the prevailing reality—
a tendency that must be overcome.

The tolerance on the part of Westerners to the inhumanity and barbarism practiced by and within their societies—as well as the active support of some for such realities—calls into question the more optimistic assertions of
the commentators examined here. Adorno may well have
been betraying Hegelian-Marxian optimism in his assertion
that he "cannot imagine a world intensified to the point of
insanity without objective oppositional forces being un-
leashed"—for the world has already descended into insanity,

and resistance can hardly be said to have been entirely un-leashed. "Hell is not something that lies ahead of us, but this very life, here and now," observes Benjamin.[113] Sociopathic oligarchs "ruthlessly creating a system of neo-feudalism and killing the ecosystem that sustains the human species," as antiauthoritarian journalist Chris Hedges puts it, are the current managers of society.[114] Progress under such condi-tions can only amount to the "first revolutionary measures taken," in Benjamin's terms, or action that works to bring about the abolition of presently constituted power.[115]

The task of bringing about a state that allows for free-dom is radically removed from the conformist orientations that allow for the election of reactionaries like members of the U.S. Republican Party—or for that matter, the U.S. Democratic Party. That openly barbarous forces are gain-ing increased control of government in many locations beyond the United States—such as Hungary, the Czech Republic, the Netherlands, the United Kingdom, and Russia—reflects a rapidly deteriorating world, although drawing conclusions about given societies from election results is not a straightforward task, given considerations, for instance, regarding participation rates or limitations on electoral choices.

If, then, as Adorno says, "anything that we can call morality today merges into the question of the organiza-tion of the world," serious questions arise about the possi-bility of morality under present conditions.[116] Acceptance of the cultural hegemony promoted by dominant groups, as in Adorno's and Antonio Gramsci's accounts, goes a long way toward explaining the absence of self-determined societies, as does the mélange of self-interest, fear, and mindlessness that perpetuates the status quo.[117] The lack of alternative societies—disenfranchisement, in Chomsky's conception—as well as generalized antisystemic movements aimed at instituting social alternatives is consistent with the continuation of radical exclusion and alienation: it condemns humanity to oblivion. In Horkheimer's words: "As long as world history follows its logical course, it fails to fulfill its human destiny."[118] Or as Holloway remarks: "Put simply, the tendency of current development is that humanity is annihilated."[119]

The task of overthrowing the present material reality and its ideological support—for humanity to debarbarize itself—is as immense as it is necessary. Unlike the end sought by Marxian science, humanity's chances are hardly ensured. "We can no longer proclaim with confidence that our victory is inevitable," writes Holloway; in Marcuse's words, "The critical theory of society possesses no concepts which could bridge the gap between the present and its future."[120] The hope, then—if there can be hope—is that social passivity and conformism will be shattered so as to allow for the "generally social democratic attitudes," which Chomsky claims are widespread among the U.S. populace, to be made more profound by means of a transition to more radically participatory political spaces.

The grounds for the hope that a reasonable and just future can be born from the present are not entirely baseless, as alarming as the threats posed to humanity by environmental catastrophe are. It is now imaginable that inclusive, egalitarian antisystemic movements will develop in

core societies, hand in hand with resistance movements
the world over, from striking Chinese industrial workers
to Arab antistatist protesters, revolutionary Kurds, Indian
Marxists, indigenous peoples, and the victims of global mil
itarism and capitalism everywhere. To continue with this
image, this multitudinous international movement could
be of and for the subordinated peoples of the world—an
egalitarian association that advances solidarity and revolutionary love. This movement would have to be wide-
ranging and diverse, taking account of human plurality
along with the various and multiple factors that perpetuate
exclusion, oppression, and unreason—such as climate catastrophe and war, in addition to neoliberal global capitalism,
patriarchy, and racism.

The point is that the means of production and social
relations must be socialized—decolonized—if barbarism
is to be averted. In this way, only through what Arendt
terms a "full experience" of the human capacity for a "new
beginning"—the faculty of interrupting what exists and
in its place "beginning something anew," like de Beauvoir's
"surpass[ing]" of "the given toward an open future"—can
hope be bestowed on the human condition.[121]

On Adorno's New Categorical Imperative

If justice perishes, the life of [humans] on Earth has no value.

—Immanuel Kant, "Justice and Punishment"

Writing in *Negative Dialectics*, his last major work, Adorno claims to have identified a "new categorical imperative" beyond that established by Kant over two centuries ago—one "imposed by [Adolf] Hitler upon unfree [humanity]": humans must "arrange their thoughts and actions so that Auschwitz will not repeat itself, so that nothing similar will happen."[1]

Auschwitz, of course, was one of the major sites erected by Nazi occupation forces in Poland that, following the institution of the *Endlösung* ("Final Solution") in 1941, served as an extermination camp for European

Jews. It is estimated that approximately a million people were murdered there by means of mass industrial killing: the infamous gas chambers and crematoriums.[2] Its genesis apparently found its basis in the relative "inefficiency" of massacres carried out by the *Einsatzgruppen* ("mobile killing units") and related groups within the Eastern European territories taken over by the Nazi war machine. This purported inefficacy arguably had to do in large part with the toll exacted on the executioners who murdered individual Jews—including women and children—as openly recognized by SS chief Heinrich Himmler.[3] Adorno's stress in his new categorical imperative on Auschwitz, then, should be taken as a stand-in for the Nazis' attempted extermination of European Jewry as a whole: the Holocaust, or *HaShoah* ("catastrophe").

In Adorno's own words, his postulated new imperative has "priority before any other requirement."[4] Being categorical, such an imperative "lay[s] claim to universal validity," as Kant's interlocutor Karl Jaspers explains.[5] It applies to us unconditionally; it is the "premier demand upon all education."[6] As a response to the breadth of the event of Auschwitz, Adorno's categorical imperative is a commentary on the centrality of the Shoah as a historical event, an expression of the "practical abhorrence of the unbearable physical agony to which individuals are exposed."[7] J. M. Bernstein notes in a study of Adorno's ethics that such abhorrence is, for Adorno, the "determining ground for *all* future action," a "reorientation" of being aimed at shaping human behavior in such a way that no one will come to experience bodily suffering of

the type brought about by the Shoah—one comparable
to Horkheimer's assertion that "suffering is the fact from
which all considerations about human life must set out."[8]
Such a reorientation would in negative terms demand the
abolition of the "aggressive nationalism" that Adorno sees
as birthing Nazism and other genocidal regimes—for example, that imposed on Armenians during the First World
War—as well as the positive institution of the generalized
social recognition that "the Jew is a human being": that
the oppressed, excluded other is an end whose interests are
to be defended and promoted. It is a call for a new humanity—one that no longer "inflict[s] [death] administratively
on innumerable people."[9]

Adorno's new categorical imperative should be taken
as a profound critique of radical exclusion and dehuman-
ization along with the very real violence that follows. It
is a continuation or even a restatement of Kant's original
imperative, which calls for humanity to be treated as an
end in itself. As such, Adorno's demand should not be read
as asserting the singularity of the Shoah, as many apolo-
gists for Israel's dispossession of the Palestinians hold, for
instance, given that his critique of Auschwitz is related
to the task of preventing the future recurrence of something "similar." His perspective in this sense is close to that
of Emmanuel Levinas, who dedicates his *Otherwise Than
Being, or Beyond Essence* to "the memory of those who were
closest among the six million assassinated by the National
Socialists" as well as "the millions on millions of all con-
fessions and all nations, victims of the same hatred of the
other man [*sic*], the same anti-semitism."[10]

As Levinas's dedication here intimates, readers of
Adorno may be skeptical about the stress in his imperative on Auschwitz, however radical an atrocity it was. The
millions of Jews killed by the National Socialist regime
were surely "denied the moral regard they deserved," in
Bernstein's words, but "such a lack of regard is massively rou-
tine in human history."[11] The destruction of the European
Jews at the Nazis' hands is for Bernstein "nothing historically or sociologically unique," but instead represents the
"direction of modern societies as a consequence of rational-
ization," the "horrific instantiation and intensification of the
dominant sociological and reflective trends of modernity."[12]
It follows from the fact of state sovereignty, under which
states claim the right to commit genocide against those subject to their dominion; the Shoah cannot be easily dismissed
as a "casual aberration of a Western world essentially sane,"
as historians Edmund Stillman and William Pfaff argue.[13]
For Polish sociologist Zygmunt Bauman, the Shoah "was
not an irrational outflow of the non-yet-fully-eradicated
residues of pre-modern barbarity" but rather "a legitimate
resident in the house of modernity," which brought about
the unchecked rule of statist bureaucracy, efficiency considerations, and scientific positivism that Bauman finds
principally responsible for the Nazi genocide.[14]

Adorno follows Max Weber's observation that the "'objective' discharge of business" performed by modern administration is carried out "without regard for persons."[15] Such
objectivization is evidenced in the subsumption of Jewish
lives to the demands of National Socialism, as in labor's
subsumption to capital, as Adorno points out. Even in the

formal freedom afforded the individual in liberal capitalist society, persons are as "replaceable as [they] will be under
the liquidators' boots," claims Adorno.[16] Such assertions—
glaring, perhaps, to those attracted to liberal politics—are
related to his interpretation of fascism's causes, which in his
view were born out of "the concentration of economic and
administrative power" by capitalism, on the one hand, and
"complete [societal] impotence on the other."[17] Bauman also
takes this position, placing the Shoah's locus in "the emancipation of the political state . . . from social control—following the step-by-step dismantling of all non-political power
resources and institutions of social self-management."[18]

With such considerations in mind, one can then ask
why Adorno stresses Auschwitz as that which must not be
allowed to recur, and why, for example, he does not identify
the barbaric genocides visited by European powers on colonized bodies decades and even centuries before the emergence of National Socialism as focal points of critique, as
was done before Adorno's time by Luxemburg and contemporarily by Arendt—with the latter, incidentally, arguing
that European colonialism served as an important model
for Hitler and his associates.[19] The world-historical near extermination of the indigenous peoples of the Americas, or
Abya Yala—the result of the European conquest, estimated
by French historian Pierre Chaunu as resulting in the death
of between forty and a hundred million people—finds
little mention in Adorno's oeuvre.[20] He pays little heed to
European society's application of fascism to non-European
peoples through imperialism, as Caribbean theorist Aimé
Césaire formulates it.[21] Nowhere does Adorno write or

speak of the "bones of defenseless Herero women . . . bleaching in the sun," as Luxemburg does in commemoration of the peoples of Namibia victimized by German imperialism, or "the death cries of martyred [indigenous] women . . . [which] fade away in the rubber plantations of the international capitalists," in Colombia as elsewhere.[22]

As is noted by U.S. Marxist literary critic Fredric Jameson, Adorno showed little enthusiasm for contemporary decolonization and anti-imperialist efforts in southern societies, in contrast, say, to his colleague Marcuse.[23] While this omission could have to do with a lack of faith on Adorno's part as regards the expected progress for southern peoples by means of formal decolonization, it is true, as Lebanese Marxist Gilbert Achcar notes, that the history of imperialism is multiple, such that "colonialist usurpation of a [given] territory" need not *ipso facto* entail "the racist extermination of whole populations."[24] Foreign domination as practiced by the Ottomans, for example, was rather different than occupation overseen by the Nazis. Still, recognition of this distinction should hardly be an excuse for Adorno's failure to concern himself centrally with the lived experiences of those subjected to European imperialism, for the inhumanity of this project should clearly have been self-evident to any observer. This tendency to overlook Frantz Fanon's "wretched of the earth" can indeed be observed as having been shared by many other contemporary Western intellectuals, even radical ones—Bookchin and Arendt not the least of these.

While it may be that Adorno's rendering invisible of the colonialism problem amounts to an omission indicative of racism, Adorno generally does not seem to have been a racist, in keeping with his concerns regarding social exclusion and authoritarianism. In his view, the atomic bombing of Hiroshima was an act reminiscent of Auschwitz and the invention of nuclear weapons "belongs in the same historical context as genocide."[25] His further opposition to racist imperial politics is seen in his denunciation of the "horror of the napalm bombs" used by the U.S. military in Vietnam and the sympathy that biographer Stefan Müller-Doohm sees him as having for those protesting the war.[26] Indeed, in his 1965 lectures on metaphysics, Adorno states that his use of the term Auschwitz should be taken to mean "not only Auschwitz but the world of torture which has continued to exist after Auschwitz," particularly as reflected in the "most horrifying reports [coming] from Vietnam."[27] While Adorno's concrete efforts to resist the Vietnam War were rather minimal in comparison with those of his more activist colleague Marcuse, and though his new categorical imperative is not, as in Anders's demand, that there be "no more Hiroshima[s]," the formulation of his imperative should be read as one demanding the total rejection of social systems responsible for the perpetuation of human suffering, as follows from Kant's original imperative.[28]

Serious efforts directed toward preventing the recurrence of Auschwitz or anything similar should likely take account of the barbarism that did in fact allow for Auschwitz and the Shoah. Explanations for the rise of Nazism and institution of the Endlösung are varied, as well as highly contentious. Neumann, for one, finds Nazism to have been the product of collaboration among Germany's industrial capitalists, governmental bureaucracy, military leadership, and the National Socialist Party. The Nazi regime in this sense was in Neumann's view a reality imposed by dominant power groups as opposed to any expression of the will of Germany's subordinated classes, which "merely follow[ed] that leadership or even resist[ed] it."[29]

In stark contrast to Neumann's conclusion here is the questionable depiction by Harvard professor Daniel Jonah Goldhagen in his *Hitler's Willing Executioners: Ordinary Germans and the Holocaust*. Goldhagen contends that National Socialism and the Shoah reflected widespread, almost primordial anti-Jewish sentiments on the part of the German people as a whole—an "eliminationist anti-Semitism" found among amorphous groups of Christian Europeans in general and particularly Germans, who are described by Goldhagen as being fundamentally anti-Semitic.[30] Goldhagen claims that such sentiments took hold of German society before Nazism, and even and especially gripped the German industrial proletariat—a rather unconvincing theory on all counts. Reviewing relevant scholarship on these questions, dissident ex-professor and activist Norman Finkelstein notes that economic considerations among Germans served as grounds for support for the National Socialist Party, and that "most Germans" did not support Nazi atrocities against Jews before the war years and even expressed outrage at such.[31] Bauman similarly finds that Germans in general did not accept the Nazis' racist propaganda, observing rightly that the historical legacy of anti-Jewish sentiments was much less extreme in Germany as compared with other European societies. Even toward the end of the war, following the hardening of many Germans to the suffering of others, it was German commoners who provided aid to Jews forced by the Nazis to engage in death marches, as Goldhagen himself recognizes. Continuing this line of thought, antifascist researcher Ruth Birn sees Goldhagen's voluntarist interpretations of the perpetration of the Shoah at the hands of "ordinary Germans" as highly problematic, agreeing instead with historical scholarship that stresses the "mixture of peer pressure, careerism, and obedience" that Goldhagen dismisses entirely.[32]

Another way to understand the rise of Nazism is Nicolas Holliman's claim in *Principia Dialectica* that the emergence of racist Nazi sociological theories, brutal imperialist expansionism, and the Endlösung would likely have not entered history had the popular revolution attempted in Germany at the close of World War I been successful rather than suppressed as it was by the Social Democrats.[33] Indeed, Germany's Social Democratic Party and the attendant lack of an autonomous labor movement must assume a great deal of the responsibility for the Nazi catastrophe. The party's hierarchical form of organizing, together with a generalized internalization of the Hegelian sense of progress propagated by the Social Democrats, may well have alienated the general populace from considering a direct confrontation with the emerging Nazi movement, as was, for instance, practiced contemporarily in Spain among radical workers. The social programs and economic stimulation provided by the National Socialist Party in response to the crippling depression also helps explain popular consent to the regime.

More fundamentally, Richard Koenigsberg's critique of the state and its ideology of nationalism is another aid in understanding complicity with fascism and mass industrial murder. In a discursive move reminiscent of Adorno and Horkheimer's assertion that the domination of nature reproduces itself through domination among humans, Koenigsberg claims that the sacrifice of millions of people in World War I served as an example reproduced by Hitler in the case of his own soldiers, on the one hand, and Jews, on the other.[34] Adorno himself similarly argues that "horror is potentially already posited" wherever the state's right is enshrined over the rights of its members—or whenever perpetrators of barbarism pass off their crimes as mere "acts of state."[35] Wilhelm Reich is similarly correct to find a social institution in the bourgeois nuclear family that generally prepares new generations for adjustment to reactionary social relations and hence perpetuates their dominance.[36] The fascist stress on traditional gender, sexual, and familial roles is well known.

Another important factor in attempting to make sense of the Nazi experience is Adorno's critique of what he terms "bourgeois coldness," or a "deficient libidinal relationship to other persons" that can be observed among "people who cannot love." He claims that, if "coldness were not a fundamental trait of anthropology, that is, the constitution of people as they in fact exist," if people in general were something other than "profoundly indifferent toward whatever happens to everyone else except for a few to whom they are closely bound," the Shoah "would not have been possible," as "people would not have accepted it." This coldness, this "indifference to the fate of others," in turn finds its basis in antagonistic, egotistical forms of social organization. Adorno views the "inability to identify with others"—this capitalist, antihumanist trait—to be "unquestionably the most important psychological condition for the fact that something like Auschwitz could have occurred in the midst of more or less civilized and innocent people."[37] The grip that such coldness seems to have held on the German social imaginary helps explain, according to Arendt, the remarkable absence of resistance on Germans' part to the Nazi regime—this in marked contradistinction to the responses of several peoples residing in spaces occupied by the Nazis, from Yugoslav and Greek guerrillas to Jewish Communist female partisans.[38] One must not forget, though, the courageous and desperate efforts of the youthful members of the White Rose to denounce fascism as well as those Germans who gave Jews refuge in their homes, however much bourgeois coldness likely synergized with popular anti-Jewish sentiments among the general German population to allow for the Shoah.

This brief review of analyses of the Nazi catastrophe, while partial and incomplete, leads to the following conclusions regarding Nazi totalitarianism: it was imposed by dominant groups and met with moderate opposition, which proved inadequate; its dominance was supported by preexisting reactionary social institutions; and its world-historical crimes were allowed to continue in part because of a marked absence of solidarity with those victimized.

While history cannot simply be said to repeat itself, social structures of domination, subjugation, and exclusion

surely do reproduce themselves, as attested to by a basic understanding of recorded human history—Hegel's slaughter-
bench. Many observers have criticized attempts to draw
parallels between happenings since the defeat of National
Socialism in 1945 and what occurred during Nazism's
twelve-year reign over Germany and much of Europe—for
example, the Bush presidency and particularly his 2003
invasion of Iraq, or Israel's treatment of the Palestinians
and other Arabs. Many of these same commentators would
likely find Bernstein's and Bauman's explorations of the po-
sitional similarity between the Shoah and other dominative
practices highly problematic.

It nonetheless must be "cried out"—á la Jacques
Derrida in his observation that "never have violence, inequality, exclusion, famine, and thus economic oppression
affected as many human beings in the history of the earth
and of humanity" as in the late twentieth century—that
the climate catastrophe currently under way is causing social exclusion, human suffering, and senseless death on a
scale for which the historical examples of Auschwitz and
the Shoah are a useful analogue.[39] Horkheimer's assertion
in 1956 that humanity is "heading for a situation compared to which Nazism was a relatively moderate affair"
surely merits consideration, especially in light of Adorno's
injunction that nothing similar to Auschwitz should be allowed to occur again.[40] The case of industrial genocide is
not dissimilar to that of nuclear annihilation, as analyzed
by Schell and others, including Adorno himself, for the
latter would amount to a "universal holocaust," to recall
Aronson.[41] It follows that there seems to be no reason not

to likewise consider the various threats posed by climate catastrophe; there is, in fact, much reason to do so.

Climate change threatens to induce severe, widespread human suffering the world over, and greatly increase the suffering imposed and overseen by capitalism. Does the desertification of formerly populated agricultural lands around the globe—eventualities entirely dependent on the use of hydrocarbons by industrial societies through their employment of capitalism and growth economies—not constitute a monstrous crime? Can the eradication of numerous Pacific island societies due to increased sea levels ever be justified, or the destruction of coastal human settlements housing the vast majority of humanity? What can be said regarding the prospect that some five million people, many of them children, are expected to die over the coming decade because of climate change, or the specter of "billion-person famines"—or indeed, the likelihood that the Andes and Himalayan glaciers, on which billions of lives depend for water, will be radically diminished by the global heating induced by capitalism—other than that everything should be done to attempt to prevent such possibilities from coming to pass?[42] An Earth that experiences climatic changes that make large areas—particularly the tropics—uninhabitable would clearly violate Adorno's new categorical imperative, as would truly apocalyptic degrees of warming (6°C–12°C, or 10.5°F–21°F) that would likely amount to what antiauthoritarian scholar Maia Ramnath terms a "final solution for humanity as a whole."[43]

Faced with such horrific possibilities, humanity can turn to the Shoah experience as a way of illuminating the current climate predicament. As has been noted, climate catastrophe could well disrupt agricultural production in much of the world, thus provoking devastating increases in malnutrition, hunger, and starvation rates, with enormous increases in human deaths. Such a possible future eventuality can be likened to the phenomenon of der Musselmänner in the Nazi camps, or inmates who had reached such a state of acute malnutrition due to their exclusion that they became little more than "staggering corpse[s]," largely incapable of expressing emotion or thought—Muslims, in the Orientalist imaginary of the imprisoned.[44] Though "still nominally alive," der Musselmänner attested to the "total triumph of power over the human being," similar to those potentially facing starvation induced by climate change.[45]

The total disregard suffered by those who became Musselmänner, alongside that shown to those who were outright murdered, speaks to the nature of the concentration camp administration. Similar observations could be made about currently prevailing administrative processes and administrators. Indeed, in light of the clearly horrendous toll that climate change stands to take on human life across the globe, the ease with which premier U.S. climate envoy Todd Stern dismisses the historical responsibility of industrial capitalist societies for the climate crisis, let alone moves toward making resources available to aid southern societies in adapting to the climate catastrophe, is in ways reminiscent of Adolf Eichmann's claim, when facing prosecution by the Israeli state for his crimes against European Jewry, that "repentance is for little children."[46] In similar terms, at the conclusion of the Copenhagen climate negotiations, Sudanese negotiator Lumumba Stanislaus Di-Aping observed that the dominant approaches endorsed by the global powers at COP—approaches radically at odds with recommendations based on established science—are based on maxims like those that "funneled six million people in Europe into furnaces."[47] In naming the accord for what it is—an agreement "devoid of any sense of responsibility or morality"—Di-Aping points to the "antireason of totalitarian capitalism," which as Horkheimer and Adorno melancholically state, "makes the satisfaction of needs impossible and tends toward the extermination of humanity."[48] Clearly, such trends have been affirmed rather than overthrown by the subsequent negotiations since Copenhagen, from Tianjin to Bonn and Cancún to Durban, and can be expected to be reproduced by policymakers at the COP18 talks to be hosted by the Qatari dictatorship in 2012 and beyond. The most recent agreement drawn up at Durban, for example, which envisions a postponement until 2020 of the institution of a new global accord to regulate carbon emissions, is nothing if not entirely authoritarian in its implications.

The radical evil represented by climate change—principally, the three hundred thousand people who die each year due to the dangerous human interference with the world's atmosphere that has already taken place as well as the various horrifying realities that global warming stands to visit on the peoples of Earth in the future—has it seems become banal, in the sense that constituted power finds little reason in the prospect of the mass suffering and death that results from climate change to recognize the present as an emergency necessitating radical action. This follows, of course, from the dominant imperatives to maintain and expand existing power structures and privileges. It represents perhaps the most extreme expression of the dominant trend within capitalist societies that valorizes capitalist profit over the interests of people—a continuation, again, of the decidedly extreme oppression historically visited on southern peoples by imperialist powers.[49]

Within the framework of a system such as this, it is largely assumed that the "normal" operation of capitalist society need not be interrupted by concerns about the continued existence of much of humanity—it is expected, indeed, that humankind and even life itself should be subordinated to the demands of capital. Such an arrangement is undoubtedly totalitarian, for it sacrifices "human freedom" to "historical development."[50] While the nameless, foreign others sacrificed by climate change are not usually referred to as a "plague bacillus" or an "epidemic" against which one must defend the interests of the fatherland or state—indeed, the victims of global warming are conspicuous for their absence in the northern imagination—the end result, which amounts to massive disregard for the welfare of the other and mass death, is not terribly different.

Dominant relations can hence be characterized as governed by what Chomsky calls a "depraved indifference" to human life.[51] Australian scientist Gideon Polya has termed the current situation "climate genocide," while Bangladeshi climatologist Atiq Rahman similarly labels it "climatic genocide."[52] These phrases are accurate if the word genocide is to be understood as murder of persons belonging to particular classes and social groups, as originally formulated by Raphael Lemkin, the concept's inventor.[53] If the definition is extended to membership or residence in particular geographic regions—a collective belonging of sorts—the term fits better, even if the question of intent for such eventualities is left unresolved: under the internationally accepted definition, acts of genocide occur only if governed by conscious intent. Against this view, Chomsky is right to suggest that those concerned with such problems focus "on predictable outcome as evidence for intent."[54] Not to work to undermine global capitalism is effectively to be complicit with the genocide of southern peoples. Jean-Paul Sartre put it well in a statement that he issued as president of the International War Crimes Tribunal on Vietnam: "The genocidal intent is implicit in the facts. It is not necessarily premeditated."[55]

The enormity of suffering threatened by climate catastrophe returns us to the most important remaining question. It is certainly the case that climate policy to date has been shaped almost entirely by power interests acting in defense of capitalism and sovereign states. It therefore could not immediately be claimed that the policies that have been practiced necessarily reflect the popular will on such matters—or to paraphrase Spanish philosopher Miguel de Unamuno, it may be that the dominant have so far been victorious, but that this victory has failed to convince those subjected to this domination. The undemocratic implications of such policy—self-evidently rather clear—lead us to the question of whether we can envision alternative policies being instituted within the near term by agents other than those who have thus far been considered responsible for such matters: Can the nonstate, which is humanity, take the place of the state in these terms?[56] Unfortunately, the U.S. public in particular is decidedly unconvinced that climate change poses serious threats to peoples' well-being now and in the foreseeable future.[57] While the attitudes of residents of other publics on this question is undoubtedly important, those of residents of the society most responsible for the climate predicament are of particular significance, for they surely influence the degree that people would be willing to undertake steps toward the radical reconstruction of society along humane ecological grounds—a crucial project that must be realized if humanity is to survive.

A great deal rests on the thought and activity of the subordinated classes of societies that can be described, like Immanuel Wallerstein does, as residing within the core of the present world system. It remains to be seen whether industrial workers who find themselves in the core will break radically with prevailing ideology and contribute to the remaking of society, as foreseen by Marx, although considerations of the observed behavior of large sections of the proletariat leave considerable room for doubt. The lack of concern and indifference often expressed for the fate of geographically distant others—such as Iraqis, Haitians, Mexicans, Bangladeshis, Palestinians, Pakistanis, and Sahelian residents—is particularly alarming, given the implications this has for international solidarity as well as the prospect of cooperative global relations and global climate rationality. The making invisible of others that is propagated by the dominant forces and accepted by the nondominant is a worrisome situation—one that must be broken radically. While Hedges may be exaggerating when he claims U.S. society to have "lost the capacity for empathy," it hardly seems to be the case that Western publics will quite literally take up arms to defend those imperiled elsewhere, as Catalunyan anarchists and others did when faced with the prospect of a fascist takeover of Spain in July 1936.[58] "The disregard for the subject makes things easy for the administration," as Adorno and Horkheimer write.[59]

Progress toward the realization of autonomous social relations presupposes the existence of autonomous individuals "capable of putting existing laws into question," as Castoriadis claims, or ones who practice what Marcuse terms an "autonomous reason."[60] Movements for autonomy and reason are alarmingly lacking across much of the globe, but particularly so in the North. It is at times as though the dominant U.S. imaginary considered other regions of the world to be a vast East that merits little investigation. It would indeed be difficult to maintain that the Western industrial proletariat has distinguished itself in its historical defense of humanity—hence the present predicament. The complicity of core publics with the destruction visited on Iraq in particular during the past quarter century has been monstrous, as has their resignation in the face of an economic system responsible for the death of millions of children annually through starvation and material deprivation. A recognition of and struggle over the "moral character of action" is missing among many who have the privilege of not personally confronting today's acute horrors, many of which are impelled by the socioeconomic system to which these people have seemingly adjusted; presumably, such individuals would act differently than they do, were they concerned about such questions.[61]

Still, such a "trend is not destiny," as environmental commentator David Orr puts it.[62] The fate of the future, though potentially catastrophic, is not yet a fait accompli; "the world's course is not absolutely conclusive," as Adorno claims, and "the horizon of history is still open," in Marcuse's words.[63] As Hardt and Negri observe, and as has been dramatically demonstrated in, say, the recent wave of popular revolts in Arab-majority societies, a "metropolis can ignite overnight"—as can a countryside or an entire region.[64]

There may be value in recalling Horkheimer's explosive assessment of Kant's original imperative as regards the relevance of Adorno's new categorical imperative to the present: "In this society of isolated individuals, the categorical imperative . . . runs up against the impossibility of its own meaningful realization. Consequently, it necessarily implies the transformation of this society."[65]

Similar conclusions follow from reflecting on Adorno's posited imperative on Auschwitz. Just as the reign of capital and the state renders impossible the generalized treatment of humans as ends, the forms of prevailing society threaten fundamentally to violate Adorno's formulated imperative. That which exists must be negated and overcome to give way to a liberated society—one that would neither engage in genocide, whether climatic or otherwise, nor take actions that would effectively destroy Earth's ability to support life. This new society would reverse the traditional reality that affords capital and the state unchecked power; instead of merely being spectators subjected to the prevailing power, participants in the construction of this new world would seek to abolish these authoritarian forms.[66] To paraphrase Camus, we must rebel so that we will continue to exist.[67] All rests on the development of an exit from the monstrous present. As Neumann declares, the system "can only be overthrown by the conscious political action of the oppressed masses."[68]

This conscious political action is seen, among other geographic-historical spaces, in the efforts of slaves in the French colony of Saint-Domingue—thereafter Haiti—to liberate themselves from domination. In Hardt and Negri's view, "Neither moral arguments at home nor calculations of profitability abroad could move European capital to dismantle the slave regimes [in Saint-Domingue and elsewhere]. Only the revolt and revolution of slaves themselves could provide an adequate lever."[69]

"The rights of human beings must be held sacred, however great a sacrifice this may cost the ruling power," writes Kant.[70] The existing system "cannot be adjusted to; like an iron collar, it can only be broken."[71]

It is to be hoped that once people reflect on and discuss climate destabilization, they will respond with sympathy, turning radically against the institutions and realities that perpetuate suffering. Such resistance is perhaps prefigured in the often-generous reactions of ordinary people to the misfortunes experienced by strangers following storms, earthquakes, landslides, and mine disasters. It is nonetheless imperative that the opposition to the causes of climate change pass from being a matter of individual charity to one of systematic resistance. Without this, the prospect for what Arendt calls a "world fit for human habitation" is difficult to conceive.[72]

Compassion—consideration of the other as a subject with interests worth valuing, defending, and promoting—then can be seen as constituting a potential exit point from the present. As Bernstein notes, compassion is a prefiguring of political justice and "anticipates the generality that justice would be."[73]

Another important consideration regarding Adorno's new categorical imperative in relation to the climate predicament is the question of responsibility—and precisely who bears it. Dyer's assertion that "nobody is to blame" is absurd; such apologism has no place here.[74]

Perhaps one of the most radical takes on responsibility for the Nazi catastrophe is the one advanced by Reich in his *The Mass Psychology of Fascism*, in which he quite bluntly states that "*the working masses of men and women, they and they alone, are responsible for everything that takes place, the good things and the bad things.*" "Under the influence of politicians," Reich maintains, people in general are led to blame particular interests for the outbreak of given wars. World War I, for example, is generally held to be the result of the actions of "munitions industrialists," while "psychopathic generals" are in this sense blamed for World War II within much of popular consciousness. Reich dismisses such explanations, equating them to a "*passing [of] the buck.*" He instead finds the "*responsibility for wars*" to fall "*solely*" on the masses of people, precisely because "*they have all the necessary means to avert war in their own hands.*" His analysis is similar for the problem of imperialism, which he finds to be both tolerated and actively supported by the masses. Due to this dynamic, however, these same forces can overthrow such phenomena dialectically. In sum, "at the bottom of the failure to achieve a genuine social revolution," asserts Reich, "lies the failure of the masses of people." The crucial point is to "activate the passive major- ity of the population, which always helps political reaction to achieve victory" and "eliminate those inhibitions that run counter to the development of the will to freedom."[75]

Arendt, in contrast to Reich, claims that the cry "We are all guilty" in fact serves to "exculpate to a consider- able degree those who actually were guilty," given, in her view, that "where all are guilty, nobody is." As she writes, there clearly were "wrongdoers" within the context of the experience of Nazism, but these people should not be seen as equivalent with the German masses as a whole. In her 1963 book *Eichmann in Jerusalem*, in particular—a work dedicated to examining Israel's prosecution of the mass- murdering Nazi bureaucrat—Arendt emphasizes thought- lessness and conformity to hierarchy as conditions that enabled as well as facilitated the prosecution of the Nazi genocide of European Jewry. In her words, "great evil" is not necessarily brought about by the machinations of a "wicked heart," which she contends is a "relatively rare phe- nomenon"; instead "most evil is done by people who never made up their mind to be either bad or good."[76] The point for Arendt is to stress the importance of obedience in any social regime. As she remarks near the close of her volume on Eichmann, "Politics is not like the nursery; in politics obedience and support are the same."[77]

The Shoah, like any other collective political effort, was a project that arose and was sustained "only out of the cooperative action of many people," together with the failures of other people consciously and practically to put an end to such barbarous forms of cooperation. Instead of colluding with negating ends, humans can in Arendt's view impede totalitarian processes by "act[ing] and interact[ing] in freedom"—by creating new and different realities that "put an end to what was there before."[78] Arendt thus calls for the prospect of the "wind of thought" to be manifest and mindlessness overthrown, for as she says only this can "prevent catastrophes."[79]

According to Adorno, the sole force capable of resisting the "principle of Auschwitz" is "autonomy," in Kantian terms: "the power of reflection, of self-determination, of not cooperating." The "very willingness to connive with power and to submit outwardly to what is stronger ... should not arise again," he writes.[80] The grounds that allow the mind the chance to "oppose the superior strength of the course of the world" are similarly found in the simple fact "that in every situation there is a concrete possibility of doing things differently," that "rebellion," in Holloway's words, "is always an option, in any situation."[81]

Naturally, the mere adoption of postures that oppose the course of the existent—idealism, in philosophical terms—will hardly suffice in light of the profundity

of the current predicament, for that which exists necessarily must be displaced in actuality. As Horkheimer
puts it, "The revolution is no good" insofar as "it is not
victorious."[82] In Merleau-Ponty's words, "victory is defeat
wherever it is not the success of a new humanity.[83]

For an Ecological Anarcho-Communism

> The bourgeoisie may blast and ruin the world they live
> in before exiting the stage of history, but we carry an-
> other world here in our hearts.
>
> —Buenaventura Durruti

From the arguments presented up to this point, it should be clear that the demands of decency and reason require a radically different world organization than presently exists. The alternative political project offered here is an ecological anarcho-communism. While the case for such a project is compelling, it does not approximate the status of a Hegelian end state or Platonic Ideal; Marcuse is right to insist that those fashioning themselves as critical theorists need to be critical of their projects and selves.[1] In the words of dissident Russian novelist Yevgeny Zamyatin's character I-330, there can be no "final" revolution, for "the number of revolutions is infinite."[2]

The social transformations that will be necessary to avert total climate catastrophe cannot emerge from conventional approaches to political questions. This should be evident to the peoples of the world after having suffered four years of the Obama administration's management of imperialist policies in the United States, for this charlatan—brought to power by means of a disconcerting degree of popular delusion about prospects for "hope" and "change"—has more than anything else simply continued the villainy of his predecessor. His numerous other crimes aside, that Obama could have nearly single-handedly dashed the hopes raised by the Copenhagen climate summit in December 2009—Copenhagen being, next to Cancún and Durban thereafter, one of official society's final attempts at pretending to address climate change—just days after defending the doctrine of imperial aggression in his acceptance speech for the 2009 Nobel Peace Prize is a reflection of the utter insanity of dominant politics. Such political forms must be radically displaced, and desperately soon, if human life is to be afforded a chance.

The problem today is that of realizing revolution—one made, as Brecht characterizes the Paris Commune, "for the sake of humanity" and in defense of life.[3] Revolution should not be taken to mean "torrents of blood, the storming of the Winter Palace, and so on"; rather, it should constitute "a radical transformation of society's institutions," as Castoriadis argues.[4] Important as such an end is in light of the climate crisis, revolution should also be understood as a means to that end.

As Arendt, Adorno, and many contemporary analysts rightly acknowledge, a great deal of confusion exists over what constitutes progress toward revolutionary ends today. In spite of such confusion, though, and in accordance with Chomsky, humanity is entirely capable of "imagin[ing] and mov[ing] towards the creation of a better society."[5] With Adorno, everyone should outwardly manifest their opposition to the world as it exists, or as Castoriadis states, "The immense majority of people who live in present-day society ought to be opposed to the established form of the institution of society."[6] While David Harvey claims in his *Enigma of Capital* that there is no "obvious way to attack the bastions of privilege for capitalist élites or to curb their inordinate money power and military might," his speculations in *Spaces of Hope* regarding the future possibility of a largely female-led "massive movement of non-violent resistance" that "neutralize[s] and eliminate[s] all weapons of violence and mass destruction" with the aim of toppling clerical-military regimes the world over may well represent the very means he seeks.[7]

Toward Ecological Anarcho-Communism

In terms of the ends served by revolution, one of the more rational ones would be an ecological anarcho-communist society. The type of social relations sought by ecological anarcho-communism would in the first place be communist—that is, a society in which Marx's principle of "from each according to ability, to each according to need" would govern economic questions, with classes and the division of labor abolished—as well as anarchist, or bereft of authoritarian social practices. Decision making could be carried out via a series of federated councils affording residents direct control of their social and economic affairs. As in Bookchin's model of libertarian municipalism, communities rather than orthodox Marxism's industrial proletarians would control production and distribution schemes—since to limit decision-making power merely to workers would be unnecessarily exclusive, marginalizing youths, older people, nonindustrial workers (such as agriculturalists), and nonworkers. Decision-making processes under such conditions would allow for the flowering of humanity's reason and compassion as well as fairly represent the interests of voiceless others, such as future generations and nonhuman animals.

Nothing in the mere existence of participatory democratic social relations, of course, would ensure such outcomes. Nevertheless, such a framework could provide the conditions under which reason and sanity would be afforded the best chance of prevailing. Takis Fotopoulos's claim that the development of a culture critical of patriarchal relations and hierarchy in general would likely "create a new ethos of non-domination" extending to the human and nonhuman world is both compelling and encouraging in this regard.[8]

An ecological anarcho-communist politics would be directed toward realizing Adorno's demand that "no one shall starve any longer"—that no one shall be denied the material conditions necessary for a dignified life. In addition, this anarcho-communism should seek to ensure social conditions under which "no one [will] fear to be different" and all will be able to engage in the "free development of each as such."[9] Radical exclusion would be overthrown, with human multiplicity and plurality seen as traits to be cherished and celebrated rather than suppressed. Patriarchy would be largely eradicated under these conditions, if not fully abolished, as would racism, ageism, homophobia, ableism, and all other conditions of unfreedom.

Anarcho-communist social relations should strive to maximize the space available for the practice of what Marx terms free conscious activity, or autonomy—a practice that can only be had in the realm of freedom, away from alienated labor. The generalized exercise of self-defined conscious inquiry would follow from the dramatic reduction of work, together with the emancipation of social relations from domination. Solidarity would serve as the basis for interrelating. Friendliness and respect would be shown to individuals. People's capacities for autonomy and creativity along with their vulnerabilities would be acknowledged. Social life would recognize the place for what Arthur Schopenhauer calls "the most necessary thing in life—the tolerance, patience, regard, and love of neighbor, of which everyone stands in need, and which, therefore, every [human] owes to [one's] fellow."[10] Individuals participating in the construction of anarcho-communism hopefully would institute the "innate repugnance" that Jean-Jacques Rousseau postulates humans experience in "seeing [their] fellow men [*sic*] suffer."[11] Chomsky's call to "deepen the emerging global bonds of sympathy and solidarity" would be similarly welcomed; such bonds, like Rousseau's pity, might help facilitate the chance for total liberation.[12]

Given that such means and ends are arguably far removed from much of what currently prevails, how might progress be made toward revolution? Barring the rapid development of a revolutionary movement, a series of thoroughgoing transitional social reforms may be needed. Three primary revolutionary reforms involve a guaranteed minimum income for all, full universal access to health care, and the decommodification of basic goods, such as food and water. Guaranteed income levels would allow working people to break from their dependence on earning a wage, and hence have greater opportunities to associate autonomously and help build social alternatives, as recognized by left-wing French philosopher André Gorz, while the second two demands would have immediate and significant impacts on health and happiness the world over.

Such changes would demand that a massive redistribution of resources from the transnational capitalist class in large part be directed at reconstructing societies devastated by disasters as well as neoliberal capitalism and militarization processes. Here one thinks of Iraq, Pakistan, Haiti, and the Democratic Republic of Congo, among other societies. One potentially transitional means toward the specific end of redistribution would be the institution of high taxes on luxury consumption, the expropriation of capitalist wealth, and redirecting the funds that presently

underpin global military spending, or simply the socialization of property and the means of production.[13] Global
nuclear disarmament—the making of the world into a
nuclear weapons and nuclear energy-free zone—could be
similarly helpful.

A future anarcho-communist society would abolish
the presently widespread practice of humans consumption of nonhuman animals; the enslavement of these animals for human purposes should be abandoned as a social
practice as much as possible. Beyond the rather inescap-
able cruelty and suffering implied by the raising of animals
for slaughter, the mass consumption of animals must be
halted or at least radically reduced in the near term on environmental grounds. Studies estimate that the industrial
processes facilitating meat consumption account for between 18 and 51 percent of the total greenhouse gas emissions produced by humanity.[14] Due to the dramatic wastefulness in the production of animal meats in terms of both
the water and grain used—surely the grain fields currently
dedicated to the feeding of cattle and other domesticated
animals, which in the United States reaches three-quarters
of the total, could more sensibly be used to feed the billions of humans who go without food—it becomes clear
that humanity should exercise conscious reason together
with compassion and abolish meat consumption to the
greatest extent possible. Adopting vegetarian or vegan
diets can in part prefigure a liberated future, as could a
broader overhaul of the industrial capitalist food system,
which sees southern societies exporting food for sale to
northern consumers while large swathes of the residents

of such societies suffer from food scarcity as their lands are bought up by transnational firms that seek to cultivate agrofuels crops there.

These measures are a few examples of action situated within current realities that would move toward ending the domination of nature—a demand as thoroughgoing as any other raised by radical, reconstructive political projects in human history. Like the abolition of patriarchy sought by feminists, the ecological society or ecological civilization presupposed here militates radically against the forces that have controlled much of human history. Without a total revolution, it is to be expected that the domination of nature would continue in an otherwise-liberated set of social relations. An anarchist society, for instance, would likely still engage in deforestation until substitutes for wood were made available. For solar energy to exist, moreover, there must also be mining, fossil fuels, and toxic waste, at least as has been practiced up to this point. Though the domination of nature can be greatly minimized through the exercise of reason along with the overturning of dominant social relations, it could live on for some time regardless of the abolition of capital and the state.

These considerations aside, much is to be gained by insisting on the critique of the domination of nature. There would be real improvements for nonhuman nature following the practices that flow from this critique. This struggle is encapsulated well in the slogan "animal liberation/human liberation" advanced by animal rights proponents. As it suggests, the project of human liberation should not exclude that of animal liberation; humans should not forget that they are animals, and that other animals have interests to be respected. As Marcuse declares, "Nature, too, awaits the revolution!"[15]

The call for an end to the domination of nature need not presuppose a lurking primitivism, whether anarcho or otherwise. That the anarcho-communism advanced here is called ecological is a reference to the sociotechnological basis for the social relations to which such a project could give birth. It would be a type of civilization—"non-repressive," in Marcuse's formulation—run on renewable, "soft" forms of energy, such as direct solar, wind, geothermal, wave, and others, that neither produce carbon dioxide, as with fossil fuels, nor threaten current and future generations with potentially terminal exposure to radioactivity, as with nuclear energy.[16] The potential for participatory, nonhierarchical societies powered along such lines that, for example, practice socialized medicine demonstrates the thoughtlessness of primitivist critics who denounce "civilization" and "technology," instead of critiquing domination and irrationality. Social ecologist Brian Tokar, for one, offers a compelling vision of "decentralized, solar-powered communities empowered to decide both their energy future and their political future."[17]

In environmental terms, the successful institution of an ecological anarcho-communism would seem to be imperative. As Hansen argues, coal emissions must be ended by 2030 if catastrophe is to be averted, with 2020 being the absolute deadline for northern societies to stop using coal altogether.[18] Li calculates that global economic growth— that is, the totality of production of capitalist value—would have to be suppressed indefinitely in the year 2015 to avoid

a 2°C (3.6°F) increase in average global temperatures.[19]
Such calculations accord with German climatologist Hans
Joachim Schellnhuber's call for the present United States
per capita release of twenty tons of carbon to be reduced
to zero tons within a decade, and with Ted Trainer's advocacy of a 95 percent reduction in consumption rates in the
industrialized North.[20]

In practical terms, Hansen advises that hydrocarbons be used consciously in the near term for the
construction of an alternative energy-production system.
Hansen's suggestion is in accordance with academics Peter
Schwartzman and David Schwartzman's March 2011 findings, which suggest that the employment of a mere 1 to 5
percent of the global total of petroleum consumed annually toward the construction of a wind- and solar-based alternative renewable energy capacity could entirely replace
existing hydrocarbon-based capacity within a matter of a
couple decades, or even more rapidly with the redirection
of greater proportions of existing capacity toward this end
as well as the institution of significant energy conservation
measures, particularly in overdeveloped northern societies.[21] Traditional U.S. environmentalist Lester Brown's
plan to reduce carbon emissions by 80 percent by 2020
bases itself principally on wind energy production as well
as rooftop photovoltaic energy, solar plants, geothermal
stations, and hydroelectric dams to a lesser degree.[22] His
plan excludes nuclear energy altogether. Writing in the
mainstream magazine *Scientific American* in 2009, Mark
Jacobson and Mark Delucchi present similar recommendations, as did the IPCC in a special 2011 report.[23] It is

in these senses that Hansen's highly questionable calls for the mass employment of third- and fourth-generation nuclear reactors to serve as base load energy to replace coal are seen as irrelevant, their irrationality having been readily confirmed once again by the 2011 disaster at the Fukushima plant, which has according to the Japanese government emitted a full one-fifth of the total radioactive material released during the 1986 nuclear disaster at Chernobyl.[24] Other estimates claim that the Fukushima plant has released even more radioactivity into the environment than Chernobyl did.[25]

Against the absurdities of nuclear energy and hydrocarbon combustion, the technological basis for averting climate catastrophe is readily at hand, and it is one that should be taken up by an ecological anarcho-communist project that would work toward the "solarization" of global society—that is, the replacement of energy resources originating in geologic solar power, or fossil fuels, with energy presently provided by the sun, whether directly or indirectly, in mimicry of the light reactions performed in photosynthesis. This movement toward solarization would be situated within the context of a more general advocacy of transition toward a steady state characterized by a closed production-consumption cycle that centrally features recycling and waste-free technologies, in accordance with David Schwartzman's vision of "solar communism."[26] A solarized global society, helped along by the institution of anarcho-communism, would then be able to observe the heretofore-violated precautionary principle, which advises against action that would harm future generations.

Assuming humanity's billions live in materially simple fashion rather than capitalistically, concentrated solar thermal plants erected in the world's deserts could readily provide for a large proportion of energy needs, as Trainer notes.[27] Alternatively, the potential in launching photovoltaic-array-laden satellites into outer space that would then transmit collected energy to Earth could be explored—a possibility raised in Elizabeth Kolbert's writings on climate change as well as Robinson's novels.[28] Space-based solar power is an intriguing option due to considerations of efficiency, given that solar collectors placed above the atmosphere receive many times the solar energy available to terrestrial solar plants, and the launching of "solar satellites" would avoid the mass erection of solar plants in Earth's deserts and thus avert the further degradation of the world's ecosystems. Whatever the potential rationality of this scheme, this project could however justifiably be met with accusations of gigantism and hence rejected. Perhaps a combination of terrestrial concentrated and photovoltaic solar, wind, geothermal, and maybe wave energy sources could instead be chosen. The newly developing self-legislating global subject will be tasked with pondering these and other alternatives.

This new constituent power should also be advised that the prospect of attaining ecologically sound ends within the near term could fruitfully be linked to the project of a postscarcity anarchism, as identified by Bookchin in the late 1960s. In postulating the possibility of a postscarcity anarchism, Bookchin claims—with Horkheimer, Adorno, and Marcuse, following Marx—that the material basis developed by the capitalist mode of production by the mid-twentieth century could, if consciously reappropriated to ends radically different than those demanded by capital, satisfy the needs of all people and drastically reduce the amount of time normally dedicated to labor under capitalism.[29] According to Bookchin, human society has for some time now been faced with the revolutionary prospect of transcending material scarcity and thus overcoming what he sees as the rationale for patriarchy, private property, class society, the state, and even hierarchy itself.[30]

Radically reorienting the productive forces and existing technologies has increased in importance since Bookchin and the Frankfurt School theorists advocated it, as the absurdities toward which production is directed live on without redress. In a very real sense, the choice humanity faces is between continuing to dedicate untold billions—even trillions—to capitalism's and militarism's most absurd and life-negating projects, or carrying out a revolutionary socialization of global society that eradicates hunger, disease, and material poverty, while also instituting a radically different energy basis for social life that does not threaten humanity with destruction. The choice is between "barbarism or freedom," observes Horkheimer, similar to the juxtaposition between socialism and barbarism that Luxemburg pointed to amid the First World War. It should be uncontroversial to state that the technological assemblage that can launch and maintain the Hubble telescope, or invent, produce, and maintain cluster bombs, stealth jet fighters, nuclear weapons, and predator drones, can also be directed at the institution of reason.

An ecological anarcho-communist political project, then, is faced with reorganizing the world—the very reconstruction of society. Though ecological anarcho-communism would demand the abolition of a great deal of prevailing practices and the transformation of dominant modes of being, it probably would not altogether abandon some of the less irrational technologies developed by capitalism. Secure interregional travel, for one, likely would not be jettisoned, though it should become more broadly accessible to the peoples of the world; communization of resources can promote this end. In place of jet airplanes—which in terms of contributions to climate change, have proven to be among the most disastrous inventions to date—a more rational society could perhaps employ air transport systems using blimps, zeppelins, and other dirigibles powered by solar energy.[31]

Another crucial infrastructural change would be a general shift toward electrically powered transportation systems—such as streetcars, railways, and electric buses—considering that the energy needed for their operation could be provided by solar or other renewable sources. Generalized short-distance transportation by bicycle could be advanced by the conscious redesign of cities. In theory, electric batteries could power cars and trucks, for if power were provided by renewable sources, the carbon-emissions problem associated with motorized transport could theoretically be solved easily. Such a resolution of course would not by itself do away with the considerable dangers posed by private automobiles to human life, as attested to by the multitudes killed annually in traffic accidents. Serious reflection on this problem may indeed demand the outright abolition of the car.

As regards water-based transportation, a prototype solar-powered vessel analogous to solar zeppelins and planes is presently under development.[32] Beyond this, water transport in a potentially liberated future could see a partial return to the employment of wind and muscle power—decolonial caravels, for example—in accordance with a reappropriation of the less destructive practices and sensibilities instituted by many humans as both individuals and groups before the historical onset of industrial capitalism—and since then. A compelling image in this sense is Japanese director Akira Kurosawa's depiction in his *Dreams* of life in a riverine village marked by social cooperation and vast diversity that is run simply on water mills.

A New International

An important means of helping along the social transformation delineated above would be through the dedicated efforts of an anarcho-communist international. Such an international—which would obviously be open to all, unlike the Marxist First International, which was largely made up of male members of the proletariat—could take as a model similar institutions, such as those established by European anarchists during the first half of the twentieth century— in particular, the Iberian Anarchist Federation (FAI) or National Confederation of Labor of Spain and Catalonia (CNT)—Koreans residing in Manchuria via the Korean

Anarchist Communist Federation in the late 1920s, and Uruguayans struggling against the capitalist military dictatorship in the latter half of the past century through the Uruguayan Anarchist Federation.[33] This critical political force could become what Chomsky calls the "first authentic International," realizing an "era of true globalization" that serves people's interests rather than those of "investors and other concentrations of power."[34] It could take the form of Hardt and Negri's multitude, consisting of an association of the various multiplicities of subordinated humans united against capital and domination, or in Negri's romantic image, "all of being and nature, the animals, sister moon, brother sun, the birds of the field, the poor and exploited humans, together against the will of power and corruption."[35]

The beginnings of such a movement can be seen, for example, in contemporary Palestine solidarity efforts— whether expressed through public protests, direct participation with the International Solidarity Movement brigades and other organizations in Palestine, or support for boycott, divestment, and sanctions campaigns against the Israeli state. It also can be found in the alter-globalization movement along with struggles against sweatshop regimes, white supremacy, sexism, police brutality, whale hunting, the prison-industrial complex, the criminalization of migration, and imperial wars. It can be discovered furthermore in campaigns in support of organic and fair trade production, among many other manifestations of ordinary people's anarchistic impulses, which are reflected "as soon as one identifies, challenges and overcomes illegitimate power," as Chomsky notes.[36]

Being anarchist, this international would have little to do with the practices of the official Internationals observed to date. The fate of the First International, which might have proven politically consequential had the rift between Marxists and anarchists not been so disastrous, arguably has much to do with Engels's redirection of its course following Marx's death. That development, in turn, was itself highly influential for the Second International, which was largely overtaken by reformist interpretations of Marx, notwithstanding the efforts of revolutionaries like Luxemburg and Karl Liebknecht, along with other members of the Spartakusbund. The Second International logically collapsed when its various national parliamentary representatives betrayed internationalism and voted in favor of the prosecution of the First World War, a social catastrophe that gave rise to fascism, both of the brown and red varieties. The repetition of all such experiences is naturally to be avoided, as are the practices of the International overseen by Vladimir Lenin and then Joseph Stalin as well as in the Trotskyist Fourth International. Doubtless, Leninism has little place as a political project both today and in the future. It cannot be said that the Bolsheviks' historical institution of the Cheka secret police, imposition of famine-inducing grain requisition regimes, repression of anarchists, destruction of the popular soviet-based government, and suppression of the Kronstadt Commune and the libertarian Makhnovshchina were defensible practices that should be resurrected.[37]

This international would oppose "the international of death" and eternal war of neoliberal capitalism, as the EZLN formulates it.[38] It would serve as the inverse to the transnational alliances made among tyrannical orders, opposing the relationship seen in the U.S. support and financing of the "third world fascism" explored by Chomsky and Herman, as evidenced in, say, Ngo Dinh Diem's Vietnam, Augusto Pinochet in Chile, Mobutu Sese Seko in Zaire, Pakistan's Muhammad Zia ul-Haq, or the Duvalier family in Haiti. The new international's practices would be far removed from the collaboration observed between Pakistani and Bahraini regimes to suppress protests in the latter country, and that practiced between the Turkish and Iranian states against Kurdish rebels; it would likely have little to do with the "mutual aid" generally expressed among highly authoritarian rulers taken in some circles to serve anti-imperialist ends—Robert Mugabe, Mu'ammar al-Gadhafi, Mahmoud Ahmadinejad, and the Chinese Communist Party, to name just a few examples. Contra Leon Trotsky, this international would never conclude that humanity is only "right with and by the [Communist] Party," as followed from his fanatic (and fantastic) belief that "history has provided no other way of being in the right"—an authoritarian self-assuredness that Arendt rightly asserts to have contributed to the totalitarian development of Bolshevik rule.[39] Instituting Roy's suggestion for a "globalization of dissent," this international would refuse the installation of rulers and sovereignty, demanding that presently constituted power fall and thereafter no person again unjustly exercise power over another.[40]

In Derrida's words, this new international could resemble

a link of affinity, suffering, and hope, a still discreet, almost secret link, as it was around 1848, but more and more visible. . . . It is an untimely link, without status, without title, and without name, barely public even if it is not clandestine, without contract, "out of joint," without coordination, without party, without country, without national community (International before, across, and beyond any national determination), without co-citizenship, without common belonging to a class.[41]

Such an institution probably could not function effectively without some sort of coordination, and this association surely should not be dominated by persons hailing from privileged backgrounds, as has been the case in many past oppositional movements, but it should certainly not be subordinated to a central party or particular national leadership, as is revealed through the troubling history of authoritarian socialism. Yet Derrida's vision here is helpful in many ways, particularly in terms of basing a movement on "affinity, suffering, and hope"—a "link" that is becoming "more visible." In place of nationalist identities propagated by the statist world system, the international could base its association on a universal solidarity among humans. Beyond a concern for human freedom, this international likely also should extend its solidarity to nonhuman life. In bringing together currents opposing domination exerted among humans as well as humanity's domination of nature, it could take after Schell's vision of a general "defensive alliance" working to protect life from the threats to survival impelled by capitalist barbarism. It could continue the work of the *"mass rising on behalf of reason"* that György Lukács sees in the historical social movements opposed to nuclear weapons, and especially in the five hundred million signatures to the 1950 Stockholm Appeal for unconditional nuclear disarmament—the very *"protection of reason as taking the form of a mass movement,"* which Lukács views as taking on a "preventive, averting character."[42] The 2011 popular uprisings, both preventive and reactive at once, aimed at reason and sanity must be carried forward. Inspiration comes from the millions of Egyptians who mobilized in Cairo's Tahrir Square and elsewhere in the country to overthrow the Mubarak regime in early 2011, as from the hundreds of thousands of Spaniards who assembled publicly to denounce the prevailing system—including, for instance, playing the *Ode to Joy* at the close of Ludwig van Beethoven's Ninth Symphony during one such gathering—and the many people who mobilized in a coordinated action worldwide on October 15, 2011, to express their support for the presently developing global antisystemic political movement.

While this oppositional mass movement may not need to turn to fiction to explore resistance efforts, the new international could consider the shadowy Human Project from Alfonso Cuarón's *Children of Men*, itself nowhere to be found in the eponymous novel by P. D. James on which the film bases itself: a group of dissident scientists purportedly based out of the Azores Islands who metaphorically labor to find a cure to the universal infertility gripping the future dystopian world depicted in the film. As in this speculative example, territorial autonomy should be an important goal for an actual movement to attain—that is, independence from the global capitalist market and state control as well as from subjection to militarism. Such an end could greatly help efforts to develop alternative rebel technologies, remake society, and launch actions against constituted power along with demonstrating the value of such an alternative. Cuba's defiance of the United States and its promotion of a more humane sort of international relations—above all in its international brigades of medical workers, but also in its material assistance for movements fighting the South African apartheid regime—has relevance in this sense, however problematic Castro's specific support for Haile Mengistu Mariam's Leninist regime in Ethiopia, not to mention the dictatorial nature of his own rule, as manifested, say, in Cuba's practice of imprisoning political dissidents as well as its historical persecution of nonheterosexuals.

The historical fact of Haiti's independence is also germane to the task of imagining this new international, given that this event was the first rebellion by slaves to successfully overthrow the forces enslaving them, however much a number of European powers (including Napoléon's France) attempted to reverse these gains by means of invasions seeking to reinstate the institution. That the uprising gave rise, as C.L.R. James reviews, to humanist notions of launching military campaigns against the slave-processing infrastructure then found in West Africa carries meaning for the present, constituting as it does a manifestation of the normally repressed revolutionary dreams of the subordinated.[43] It is also worth noting the particularly radical decolonization of South Yemen (later the People's Democratic Republic of Yemen), which brought a nominally Marxist regime to power that in contradistinction to many other putatively "socialist" polities in the Middle East and beyond, engaged in significant redistribution schemes and public health improvements domestically even as it actively aided groups working to overthrow reactionary bourgeois Arab governments in the Gulf region—despite its problematic professed democratic centralism.[44]

In recent years, Wikileaks has done significant work to expose the madness and brutality of dominant power, and thus is justifiably a beacon for the disenfranchised everywhere. Its release of documents on the U.S. ambassador to Tunisia arguably contributed to the outbreak of popular revolt in that country following Mohammed Bouazizi's self-immolation in December 2010, and its publication of a cable detailing a U.S. military massacre of Iraqi civilians was instrumental in the Iraqi state's refusal to allow occupying U.S. troops immunity from prosecution—a development that catalyzed the general withdrawal of troops from that country.[45] Through its checks on constituted power, this regulative anarchic body has contributed immensely to the struggle against hegemony, generally informing global publics of the myriad crimes of global capitalism, from the details regarding U.S. military death squads to intimidation and coercion as practiced by stronger states against less powerful ones in climate negotiations and the United States' opposition to international treaties banning the use of cluster munitions.[46]

It is unfortunate, though unsurprising, that the authorities have hampered Wikileaks' work, but it would seem that this fate follows from the organization's dependence on its founder and editor Julian Assange, who for all his importance is readily suppressed by the state and capital—as his alleged assistant, Private First Class Bradley Manning, infamously has been. Perhaps more promising in this sense is the more decentralized model exercised by anarchic hacking groups such as Anonymous and Anti-Sec, which, like Wikileaks, collaborate to disrupt the functioning of existing power.

With regard specifically to climate catastrophe, the efforts of this new international probably should intertwine with those promoted by such international radical ecological associations as Climate Justice Action, Rising Tide, the Mobilization for Climate Justice–West, and Climate S.O.S. Some of the key tasks of this international would overlap with Climate Justice Action's primary demands, which include working to prevent the future exploitation of fossil fuels, massively reducing northern consumption patterns, recognizing the Global North's ecological debt, and concurrently making reparations available to southern societies for the crimes of colonialism, neoliberal capitalism, and climate destabilization. Against the seemingly "boundless imperialism" driven by mindless capitalist modes of being, participants in the international could advance Warner Sachs's model for a "politics of sufficiency" by promoting the generalized adoption of simpler, less materially intensive lifestyles among northern residents.[47] Beyond this, and more concretely, it could work toward the appropriation of a federated series of territorial commons in which social and physical autonomy is to be developed, renewable energy infrastructures constructed, and mass reforestation and afforestation campaigns advanced, with this last perhaps following Wangari Maathai's model. In its rejection of dominant policy, the new international could reflect and amplify the radicality of the movements contesting dams that have organized politically from South Asia to Latin America.

In philosophical terms at least, this new association should avoid the racist assumptions that have informed a great deal of Western environmentalism to date. This includes, especially, the Malthusianism that faults southern high population growth rates rather than capitalism for human suffering and environmental destruction, as well as the continued advocacy of nuclear energy, which unavoidably disregards the oppressed peoples who disproportionately suffer the effects of nuclear waste, whether Native Americans or Somalis, to say nothing of those directly exposed to radioactivity emitted by malfunctioning reactors. Exercising reason and compassion, the builders of this international would promote the dissemination of antisystemic perspectives on prevailing society, and generally work to implement the vision of a global society freed from the reproduction of capitalist value and social domination.

The new international also would strive to (re)activate the *potenza*—potential—of the constituent power represented by the subordinated human multitudes of the world, working for the counterpower or dual-power model of humanity against the concentrated power of capital and the state (*potere*). This social antagonist model, advocated by a number of anarchist thinkers, has been observed historically in forms of directly democratic government as temporarily and partially realized, for instance, in the events of 1871, 1905, 1936, 1956, and 1968; as prefigured in the U.S.-based Movement for a New Society during the last quarter of the twentieth century; and arguably as practiced in the Russian agrarian *mir* system and perhaps the village councils of traditional India.[48]

Continuing the examples set in recent memory by the popular rebellions that have erupted across the world, the international's constituent parts would work to simultaneously construct popular participation in sociopolitical matters and seek to interfere with the institutions and processes that imperil life. The former end is seen in the task of devolving power to the global demos, as Arendt, Chomsky, and Bookchin advocate, and in the project of constructing and appropriating the commons as well as through broadly communal and sympathetic ways of interrelating. The work of disrupting prevailing power relations can be envisioned in direct action against spaces that are especially destructive in environmental terms, the efforts of international brigade groups—medical and otherwise—that seek to provide solidarity with and care for those abandoned as well as destroyed by capitalism, and a generalized advocacy of and political organizing toward the realization of a general strike along with popular social revolution to overthrow capitalism and the state.

The direct action that members of the international could both promote and engage in would continue the work of Plane Stupid, the Kingsnorth Six, and other UK-based radical environmental groupings that have consciously intervened against air travel and coal-based energy production in recent years as well as the sustained mass protests seen in 2011 in India's West Bengal, Maharashtra, and Tamil Nadu states against the planned construction of nuclear plants.[49] To turn to fiction again, the international could look toward the example of the Central American rebels found in John Brunner's *The Sheep Look Up* who actively disable the operations of polluting factories. It could gain insight from the factual shuttering of the Dalian petrochemical complex in northeastern China, propelled as it was by popular mobilizations on the part of hundreds of thousands opposed to its continued operation, and the concessions made by the German state in its recent pledge to close all nuclear plants within a decade following mass street protests in that country in the wake of the Fukushima disaster.[50]

Toward the end of presenting a serious challenge to prevailing power relations, this new international critically should seek to avoid the depressingly unproductive squabbling that has long plagued many interactions among libertarian socialist theorists and actors. Bookchin's rather baseless invective directed at the Frankfurt School theorists comes to mind here—he bizarrely claims these thinkers "in no sense" to be "resolutely critical of hierarchy and domination"—as does his irrational denunciations of Takis Fotopoulos and the

inclusive democracy project for their "subjectivism."[51]
Hardly innocent themselves, proponents of the inclusive democracy project have in fact perpetuated such
infighting, as is seen in the hostility at times evinced by
these to the thought of Castoriadis and Chomsky—directed toward the latter for the purported statism seen
in his open support for Medicare, Medicaid, and other
basic social welfare programs provided by the U.S. government. This problem, indeed, seems to extend from
anarchist theorists to anarchist actors. One observer
of the present Greek anarchist movement notes that
the various differences among distinctly self-identified
Greek libertarians has to an extent discouraged common
revolutionary efforts.[52]

Naturally, dissent is important, and it is arguably
more crucial now than at any other point in human history: human survival is intimately linked with the prospect of rebellion, as Camus notes. This should not mean,
though, that thinkers and other agents associated with
radical political projects should themselves reproduce
much of the fragmentation that permeates mainstream
institutions by either refusing respectfully to consider the
work of theorists and action of activists with whom they
justifiably share a great deal of concern or dismissing them
altogether for not sharing their precise views on every
given question. This is not to say that social anarchists
should suspend their opposition to Leninist politics or
desist from critiquing primitivist and individualist currents that refuse to engage with collective efforts in search
of liberation.[53]

Forward the Global Revolution

*Revolutionary transformation has a tradition that must
continue.*
—Max Horkheimer, "The End of Reason"

The miracle that save the world . . . from its normal,
"natural" ruin is ultimately the fact of natality.
—Hannah Arendt, *The Human Condition*

In general terms, reflection on human history and global
society necessarily reveals a seemingly limitless diversity
of sociopolitical practices among different groups and individuals across both space and time. This understanding,
one of the central points advanced by Karl Polanyi in his
The Great Transformation, is a significant one, echoed by
Arendt's emphasis on human plurality, "embodied" as it is
"in the absolute difference of all [humans] from one another."[54] Contemplation of such plurality, as of art or natural
beauty, can serve as a source of inspiration for revolutionary
action in the world, especially when one considers that this
plurality—like art, beauty, or the world entire—is imperiled as it is by the specter of the perpetuation of capitalism
and domination.

Briefly, then, this final section takes account of a
few noteworthy antisystemic projects and developments,
both contemporary and historical. This examination is
necessarily partial and limited.

Following the collapse of the Soviet Union along with the attendant marginalization of leftist thought and action in official circles, the Ejército Zapatista de Liberación Nacional (EZLN) represented one of the most inspiring political developments at the time. Based in the highly impoverished state of Chiapas, Mexico, the EZLN began as a guerrilla group among excluded, largely landless indigenous peoples residing in the jungles of the eastern part of the state. Its insurrection on January 1, 1994—the outcome of the democratic exercise of the voice of EZLN base communities, and a reflection of recognition among the guerrillas that resorting to conventional political methods could offer them no solution—was met with fierce repression by the Mexican authorities, although this was tempered by rapid protest mobilizations undertaken through much of Mexico and internationally. Since it emerged on the world stage in 1994, the movement has been targeted by the Mexican military, state-supported paramilitary groups, and developmentalist counterinsurgency strategies, as taken up in much of Chiapas by Mexico's various governments.

Despite these challenges, the neo Zapatista movement—"neo" because it extends the tradition of the largely indigenous Ejército Libertador del Sur led by Emiliano Zapata during the Mexican Revolution—has doubtlessly distinguished itself in its defense of humanity. This is evident in its efforts since 1994 and before to create spaces promoting autonomy and dignity, by means of the establishment of educational systems and health clinics, the stress on women's liberation campaigns under traditional indigenous patriarchal settings, physical resistance to global capitalism in affirmation of humanity and its will to live, advocacy of a communal effort by all those "from below and to the Left" to remake Mexican and global society outside electoral politics (La Otra Campaña, or the Other Campaign), thoughtful intervention and critique regarding political matters in Mexico, and opposition to Israel's murderous assaults on Gazans, among many other advances. The international meetings held in neo-Zapatista communities in the 1990s are considered legendary, given such titles as the Intercontinental Meeting for Humanity and against Neo-Liberalism, considering the righteous declarations and communiqués that resulted from them. That few such meetings have been held in recent years is unfortunate, itself perhaps an expression of the movement's decline, as arguably was reflected in the EZLN's two-year period of silence from 2009 to 2011, as well as the reported abandonment of the movement by many former members faced with impoverishment, on the one hand, and statist repression, on the other.

If it is true that the neo-Zapatista movement is in decline, this would amount to a significant loss for humanity, for the Zapatista emphasis on direct confrontation with power, opposition to inhumanity, participatory democracy, social inclusion, and international solidarity certainly all remain highly relevant for the present and likely future. Dissident writer Ramor Ryan, echoing his comrade Niels Barmeyer's criticism of the movement, is correct to note that many Zapatista adherents are disappointingly "authoritarian, patriarchal, and conservative" in the flesh.[55] Whatever the fate of the EZLN and its supporters, its politics clearly have roused the revolutionary passions of countless persons, from autonomous youths and proletarians in Mexico, to privileged Europeans who accompany the movement as international observers. As with other revolutionary insurgencies, the neo-Zapatista demand for dignity will not soon be forgotten. Perhaps it can be synthesized to a more generalized movement, in accordance with the EZLN's call to "be a Zapatista wherever you are."

On Mexico's national stage, there have been mass protests in opposition to the violence of Calderón's drug war, including an April 2011 mobilization in Mexico City titled "*Estamos hasta la madre!*" ("We are fucking fed up!"). The Movement for Peace with Justice and Dignity, born within this moment of upheaval, has rather significantly given a voice to the countless thousands whose lives have been shattered by the conflict, via its series of caravans to different regions of the country affected by the violence. The movement's proposal for a "citizen's pact" among subordinated Mexicans is an encouraging development, notwithstanding the reformist vision of the movement's official leadership and the highly questionable decision to open negotiations with Calderón in an effort to raise his awareness of the human implications of his war strategy. This sort of tactic has shown itself to be absurd on countless occasions, whether during the petitioning by Saint Petersburg's urban poor of Czar Nicholas II in January 1905 or in McKibben's 2010 "Solar Road Trip" to present Carter-era solar panels to the Obama White House.

The Kurdish Workers' Party (PKK), which arose in the last quarter of the twentieth century among the Kurds of the Near East—the largest grouping of stateless people in the world—embodies a quite different approach from the Gandhian attempts to humanize oppressive power structures. This Leninist organization, founded by Abdullah Ocalan, emerged in response to the plight of dispossessed Kurds and the widespread recognition that even nominally leftist currents in Turkey—the state of residence for the majority of the Kurds—would not prioritize a just solution to their exclusion—a position confirmed by the worldwide silence about the genocidal al-Anfal campaign prosecuted by Saddam Hussein against Kurdish populations at the end of his war with Iran in 1988. Abandoned, the PKK initiated armed struggle against the Turkish state and, in turn, met with fierce repression by the Turkish government, which in the 1990s destroyed countless villages and forcibly displaced some million Kurds as part of its counterinsurgency strategy.[56] The struggle continues, thirteen years after Ocalan's capture and imprisonment, with little progress toward the independent state sought by the PKK. Turkey, which presents itself as a progressive alternative to collaborationist Arab regimes as regards Israel and the Palestinians, and donates generously to victims of famine in Somalia, still bombards Kurdish positions indiscriminately to this day.

Despite the Kurdish people's suffering, an uncritical celebration of the PKK would be out of order, given its quasi-Stalinist nature, forced conscription, and exclusion and even murder of those who disapprove of its methods. Yet it is undeniable, even in light of the unpalatable aspects of its praxis, that the PKK's genesis has to a degree aided in the struggle against patriarchy in Kurdish society,

considering the honored participation of women in PKK
ranks, in addition to the party's importance as a source of
dignity and self-respect for oppressed Kurds.[57] As with the
Zapatistas of Mexico and the Naxalites of India, it is in
the strength of the PKK's "No saying" to domination and
abandonment that its significance is apparent.[58] The PKK's
example hopefully will be developed in the future into a
more legitimate model for the Kurds themselves, not to
mention other peoples. Perhaps Ocalan's recently expressed
interest in Bookchin's work is indicative of a new direction
for the Kurdish struggle.

In contrast to all Leninist models, the civil unrest in
2011 throughout much of the Middle East and North
Africa seems to hold more promise, despite the brutal responses of the existing regimes as well as the discouraging
lack of material progress beyond symbolic change. Zine
el-Abidine Ben Ali, Hosni Mubarak, and al-Gadhafi have
been deposed. Radical interventions by masses of people
have proven central in the cases of Tunisia and Egypt;
similar interventions aimed at overturning the status quo
have followed in Bahrain, Yemen, Syria, Sudan, Palestine,
Ethiopia, Swaziland, Angola, and many other societies.
The millions who participated in what has been termed the
Tahrir Commune in Cairo, in addition to those other millions who mobilized elsewhere in Egypt against Mubarak's
rule after the beginning of the revolutionary movement
on January 25, 2011, attest to the collective strength of
the human multitude—its capacity for resisting brutality and instituting different relations. The recent uprisings
draw from the 2007 industrial strikes in Mahalla and the

2003 mass mobilizations in Tahrir against the impending U.S. invasion of Iraq, themselves echoes of the Palestinians' resistance in general, and the First Intifada in particular. Practices like those observed in the self-management of Tahrir Square, popular and neighborhood committees in Tunisia and Egypt, and autonomous mobilizations in Cairo to protect museums from looting are undoubtedly anarchistic in nature, whatever the expressed political preferences of the participants.

The efforts taken by the post-Mubarak Supreme Council of the Armed Forces in Egypt, themselves backed by imperialism, are aimed at suppressing dissent and containing the prospects for social change. Hence the Egyptian military's ban on strikes, its multiple violent attacks on protesters assembled in Tahrir Square, its imprisonment of thousands of dissidents, and its October 2011 massacre in Cairo of Christian Copts protesting their marginalization. The movement's reactivation after January 25 is seen in the ongoing mobilizations calling for a "second revolution" (*thawra al-thania*) against the Supreme Council of the Armed Forces and Field Marshall Mohammed al-Tantawi—reminiscent in a way of the third revolution sought by proletarians and peasants in the early years of the Bolshevik dictatorship. It bears reflection that Mubarak fell just as Egypt's industrial workers initiated a general strike; the generals, like the transnational capitalist class, similarly fear these potentialities. They do not want to see the Egyptian people's resolutely anti-imperialist views manifested in reality through any sort of autonomous policy determination, and they do not favor the prospect of a democratic opening that would most likely develop in anticapitalist directions, given neoliberal capitalism's responsibility for the mass privation generally suffered by the Egyptian people and the substantial increases in food prices that have only added to the grievances.[59]

Such considerations help explain the junta's effective alliance with the Wahhabite Muslim Brotherhood, before and after the 2011 elections: better close ties with known reactionary forces than the promises of critical democratic praxis realized by the radical youth movement that has been seminal throughout this revolt. As Samir Amin notes, Egyptian Wahhabism is likely the influence of twentieth-century Saudi Arabian oil wealth and the propagation of reactionary views throughout the countryside by the land-owning classes. Amin opposes the practice of Egyptian Wahhabism—indisputably violent and oppressive, as can be seen in Wahhabite attacks on Copts in the weeks predating January 25, as in the Islamist collaboration with the military during its October 2011 attacks on Copts—to the historical tradition of Egyptian Sufism, a less hierarchical interpretation of the religion.[60] This relationship to Sufism also seems to exist in Pakistan, another society that has met with undue Saudi Wahhabite interference in recent decades, thereby following the pernicious tendency toward fundamentalist Islamization, which is itself a response to the decline of nationalist and socialist movements throughout southwestern and South Asia.[61]

In India, the world's largest country by population, a multitude of resistance projects have held sway for some time, from the 1857 Sepoy Mutiny to the decolonization movement and the postcolonial Naxalite insurrection. The communist revolt in the Telangana region of the state of Hyderabad shortly after formal independence sought to bring about a Red India by mobilizing the country's impoverished mass of peasants.[62] The land redistribution schemes engaged in by the Telengana rebels in favor of the peasantry were seminal for the later development of the Naxalite movement, as were B. R. Ambedkar's efforts to organize in favor of India's Dalits, not to mention that of the Dalit Panthers themselves.[63] The Communist Party's rule in the states of West Bengal and Kerala is perceived as having provided a more egalitarian, less environmentally destructive approach to development after independence; women's rights in particular appear to be more respected specifically in Kerala than elsewhere in the country, as are the rights of the poor.

This situation contrasts markedly with that of the country's center and east, home to the indigenous adivasi peoples whose very lands and lives are threatened by unprecedented planned mining projects that seek to remove the trillions of dollars' worth of bauxite from the mountains in which they reside.[64] Binayak Sen, imprisoned in 2007 by the Indian state for his activism in favor of the adivasis, is not mistaken in claiming such plans to be genocidal. Qualified support thus should be given to the Naxalite movement, a Maoist grouping comprised of adivasis and middle-class Hindus alike that has taken up arms against the Indian state in defense of the impoverished and marginalized. However problematic the politics of the movement's founder, Charu Mazumdar, who advocated terroristic annihilation campaigns directed against India's privileged, its historical ties to Chinese Communism, which resulted in silence on its part regarding China's dispossession of Tibet and the ravaging of Bangladesh by China's ally Pakistan, and its undeniable violent excesses, it has established a countersociety within the Dandakaranya forest in which the landless are afforded land and women are granted more respect.[65] Beyond this, it is a symbol of dignity and self-respect for the oppressed of India, quite similar in this sense to the EZLN or PKK. As Roy writes, the Naxalites have "kept the dream of revolution *real* and present in India."[66] Without that dream, she implies, matters would be far more bleak than they are—given that there are more impoverished people in eight of India's states than in the twenty-six countries that comprise Africa south of the Sahel, that 1.5 million Indian children die in their first year of life, and that hundreds of thousands of peasants have committed suicide in recent years to escape their debts.[67]

Beyond these contemporary and historical examples lies the lived experience of what Bookchin terms "organic societies," or those groups derided by anthropological racism as "primitive." As anthropologists Marshall Sahlins, Lewis Henry Morgan, and Pierre Clastres have shown convincingly, many such societies have instituted maxims radically different than those that prevail within capitalist societies: acephaly (the absence of hierarchy), individual autonomy, and substantive time freed from work. Engels's exploration of generalized sexual promiscuity and group marriage before the family's historical rise is an important recognition of radical social alternatives within human culture.[68] Bookchin's enthusiasm for the ethics of complementarity and an irreducible minimum identified by Paul Radin as practiced in some organic societies—the irreducible minimum referring to the inviolable provisioning of the basic necessities of life to each member of a given social group without regard to one's productive contribution, or Marx's "primitive communism"—hardly seems misplaced today in light of the radical mass deprivation overseen by capitalism as well as that which catastrophic climate change would bring about. That there is little evidence for the existence of war prior to the rise of agriculture and states—war being defined in Douglas Fry's review on the question as political violence directed against out-groups—is also encouraging.[69] Albert Einstein is then right to celebrate the socioeconomic practices exercised by many indigenous and organic social groups as demonstrating that "human beings are not condemned, because of their biological constitution, to annihilate each other or to be at the mercy of a cruel, self-inflicted fate."[70]

Considered together with the efforts of political resistance groupings, the historical and contemporary existence of such societies shows, in Adorno's words, that "this hell . . . cannot be the last word."[71] Clastres speculates that stateless humanity prevented the emergence of the state for hundreds of thousands of years by murdering those individuals who aspired to hierarchical power. Yet such an approach likely would be problematic if applied as a means of addressing the present situation. As

Agamben argues, "No ethics can claim to exclude a part of humanity, no matter how unpleasant or difficult that humanity is to see."[72]

However unpalatable political murder may be, some means of overthrowing prevailing power arrangements must be taken desperately soon. Borrowing from Michel Foucault, we must symbolically cut off the king's head while also metaphorically destroying the guillotine, as the Parisian Communards did promptly after taking power in March 1871.[73] Toward this end, it should be self-evident that a mere exodus from statist domination on the model of the nonhierarchical societies established by fugitive state captives fleeing the rice-growing kingdoms of lowland Southeast Asia for the stateless highlands known as Zomia, or runaway Brazilian slaves setting up *quilombos*, are insufficient strategies, for they erroneously assume that one can escape capitalism without directly confronting it with the aim of also abolishing it.[74] Whether progress toward the end of instituting revolution would demand a temporary withdrawal into an underground—as modeled, for example, historically by the neo-Zapatistas during the decade of preparation before January 1994 and speculatively by the liberatory resistance movements imagined in Robinson's *Mars* trilogy—is not something that can be resolved here, other than to note that there likely is not enough time left, environmentally speaking, for dissident organizers and thinkers to break ties with the rest of society for any significant period. What can be said is that presently constituted power must be overthrown. Capital accumulation, as Harvey declares outrightly, "will have to be stopped," and the capitalist class, "which will never willingly surrender its power," necessarily will have to be dispossessed of its "property, wealth, and powers."[75]

The radical violence, alienation, and destructiveness overseen and directed by prevailing power is but the continuation of long-standing social trends that have gone on for millennia—totalitarianism grew out of imperialism and capitalism, while hierarchy has been sustained by patriarchy and religion.[76] Most important is the understanding that the current forms of world alienation, humanity's "societal constitution," jeopardize its very existence. Considering this situation, openness to historical alternatives becomes a necessity, given the consequences that will follow without the institution of social relations radically different than present ones. The impetus to remake the world along different lines is now the only means by which total catastrophe can reasonably be avoided.

As this work has examined, though, the prospect that humanity will fail to radically reconstruct global society on humane ecological grounds within the near term is entirely within the realm of possibility. Catastrophic climate change threatens humanity's well-being in a manner perhaps even more extreme than that posed by nuclear arms—and the threat of a synergy between these two forces is decidedly more frightening than consideration of either of the two alone. Nevertheless, barring mechanical failures or mistakes, the offensive employment of nuclear weapons ultimately depends on human choice at a certain point, whereas the laws of atmospheric physics have no such potential fail-safe mechanism. The atmosphere, as is correctly observed by Earth scientist Andrew Glikson, is not "waiting for human decision."[77] It responds to humanity's mutilated forms in keeping with scientific predictions based on the laws of chemistry and physics; it has been subjected to destabilization processes graver than those imagined by even the most pessimistic accounts. While sectors of humanity continue to blind themselves to the realities of climate change and the relatively privileged fail radically to act in the interests of well-being, reason, and survival, "glaciers continue to retreat, new hazards keep emerging, and water sources dwindle."[78] In short, world alienation barrels life on toward the abyss.

This world alienation, a term first used by Arendt to describe capitalist wealth accumulation processes that demand as a precondition of their functioning that "the world and the very worldliness of [humankind] are sacrificed," follows from the historical rise of the capitalist mode of production, the division of Earth's territory into sovereign states, and the historical failure to date to overturn the monstrous system that upholds both such interrelated systems.[79] Given such conditions, one may succumb to overwhelming despair regarding the human prospect and thus withdraw from engagement with politics entirely. It has been the argument advanced here—indeed, one of the very bases of the writing of this book—that such despair should not be total. As Adorno writes, "The world's course is not absolutely conclusive, nor is absolute despair; rather, despair is its conclusiveness."[80] Human society after all is the product of its myriad constituent parts, which are not limited to capital and the state. These barbaric forms do not have the final word.

The prospect of an exit from social and environmental barbarism depends critically on the autonomous action of the subordinated. This social force has a responsibility to resist dominant socialization processes that would perpetuate existing relations in favor of realizing the imperative for social revolution—the only means by which humanity as a whole can come to be treated as an end in itself and by which climate catastrophe can be averted.

Notes

Prologue

1. Suzanne Goldenberg, "Last Year Was Joint Warmest on Record, Say Climatologists," *Guardian*, January 12, 2011.

2. John Vidal, "Carbon Levels Hit New Peak, Research Shows," *Guardian*, May 31, 2011.

3. Peter D. Ward, *The Flooded Earth: Our Future in a World without Ice Caps* (New York: Basic Books, 2010), 63.

4. Fiona Harvey, "Worst Ever Carbon Emissions Leave Climate on the Brink," *Guardian*, May 29, 2011.

5. Steve Connor and Michael McCarthy, "World on Course for Catastrophic 6° Rise, Reveal Scientists," *Independent*, November 18, 2009.

6. Gaia Vince, "One Last Chance to Save Mankind," *New Scientist*, January 23, 2009.

7. Jenny Fyall, "Warming Will 'Wipe Out Billions,'" *Scotsman News*, November 29, 2009.

8. David Harvey, *The Enigma of Capital* (Oxford: Oxford University Press, 2009), 185.

9. Imperial College London, "Asteroid Killed Off the

Dinosaurs, Says International Scientific Panel," *Science Daily*, March 4, 2010; Juliette Jowitt, "Humans Driving Extinction Faster Than Species Can Evolve, Say Experts," *Guardian,* March 7, 2010.

10. Suzanne Goldenberg, "Planet Earth is Home to 8.7 Million Species, Scientists Estimate," *Guardian*, August 23, 2011.

11. George Wilhelm Friedrich Hegel, *Lectures on the Philosophy of World History: Introduction*, trans. Hugh Bar Nisbet (1828; repr., Cambridge: Cambridge University Press, 1975), 118, 131–40; Félix Guattari, *The Three Ecologies*, trans. Ian Pindar and Paul Sutton (London: Athlone, 2000), 28.

12. Max Horkheimer and Theodor W. Adorno, *Dialectic of Enlightenment: Philosophical Fragments*, trans. Edmund Jephcott (1947; repr., Stanford, CA: Stanford University Press, 2002), xviii, 1.

13. Guattari, *The Three* Ecologies, 45.

14. Herbert Marcuse, *One-Dimensional Man* (Boston: Beacon Press, 1964), 16; Karl Marx, introduction to *Contribution to the Critique of Hegel's Philosophy of Right*, ed. Joseph O'Malley (Cambridge: Cambridge University Press, 1982) (translation modified; emphasis in original).

15. Hannah Arendt, *Responsibility and Judgment*, ed. Jerome Kohn (New York: Schocken Books, 2003), 259.

16. Hegel, *Lectures on the Philosophy of World History*, 69 (translation modified).

17. Albert Camus, *Caligula and Three Other Plays*, trans. Stuart Gilbert (New York: Vintage, 1958), 245.

18. Steve Connor, "Melting Greenland Glacier May Hasten Rise in Sea Level," *Independent*, July 25, 2005.

19. Karl Marx, *Capital: A Critique of Political Economy, Vol. 1*, ed. Frederick Engels, trans. Samuel Moore and Edward Aveling (1867; repr., New York: Modern Library, 1906), 709.

20. Ciro Pérez Silva, "Anuncia Calderón programa para sustituir los focos incandescentes por ahorradores," *La Jornada*, December 7, 2010.

21. "No se descuidarán los patrullajes en la ciudad: Seguridad Pública," *Por Esto! de Quintana Roo,* November 27, 2010.

22. "Equipan a la policía municipal," *Por Esto! de Quintana Roo*, November 28, 2010.

23. Mike Gonzalez, "Evo Morales's Defence of Mother Earth Rings Hollow in Bolivia," *Guardian,* October 3, 2011.

24. Polly Higgins, *Eradicating Ecocide* (London: Shepheard-Walwyn, 2010); see also Polly Higgins, "Why We Need a Law on Ecocide," *Guardian*, January 5, 2011.

25. Christos Filippidis, "The Polis-Jungle, Magical Densities, and the Survival Guide of the Enemy Within," in *Revolt and Crisis in Greece*, ed. Antonis Vradis and Dimitris Dalakoglu (Oakland, CA: AK Press, 2011), 69.

26. Hegel, *Lectures*, 69; Hannah Arendt, *On Revolution* (1963; repr., New York: Penguin, 2006), 62.

27. John Vidal, "Climate Change Will Devastate Africa, Top UK Scientist Warns," *Guardian*, October 28, 2009; Ward, *The Flooded Earth*, 106; Mike Davis, "Living on the Ice Shelf: Humanity's Melt Down," in *The Green Zone: The Environmental Costs of Militarism*, ed. Barry Sanders (Oakland, CA: AK Press, 2009), 7–17.

28. Jason Samson, Dominique Berteaux, Brian J. McGill, and Murray M. Humphries, "Geographic Disparities and Moral Hazards in the Predicted Impacts of Climate Change on Human Populations," *Global Ecology and Biogeography* 20, no. 4 (July 2011): 537.

29. Justin Sheffield and Eric F. Wood, *Drought: Past Problems*

and Future Scenarios (London: Earthscan, 2011), 180–83.

30. John Vidal, "Global Warming Causes 300,000 Deaths a Year, Says Kofi Annan Thinktank," *Guardian*, May 29, 2009.

31. Dara and Climate Vulnerable Forum, *Climate Vulnerability Report 2010*, available at http://daraint.org/wp-content/uploads/2010/12/CVM1.pdf.

32. Noam Chomsky, *Hopes and Prospects* (Chicago: Haymarket Books, 2010), 133.

33. Albert Memmi, *The Colonizer and the Colonized* (Boston: Beacon Press, 1965), 62.

34. Hannah Arendt, *The Origins of Totalitarianism* (1951; repr., San Diego, CA: Harcourt, 1968); Herbert Marcuse, *Negations: Essays in Critical Theory*, trans. Jeremy J. Shapiro (Boston: Beacon Press, 1968), 19.

35. Max Horkheimer, "Die Juden in Europa," *Zeitschrift für Sozialforschung* 8 (1939): 115 (translation from Fredric Jameson, *Late Marxism: Adorno, or the Persistence of the Dialectic* [London: Verso, 1990], 113).

36. Theodor W. Adorno, *Minima Moralia: Reflections on a Damaged Life*, trans. E.F.N. Jephcott (1951; repr., London: Verso, 1974), 80; Dara and Climate Vulnerable Forum, *Climate Vulnerability Report 2010*.

37. Karl Marx, "Letter from Marx to Arnold Ruge," in *Karl Marx and Frederick Engels: Collected Works* (Moscow: International Publishers, 1975), 1:393–95.

38. Theodor W. Adorno, *Critical Models*, trans. Henry W. Pickford (New York: Columbia University Press, 2005), 298.

39. "Famine Spreads to Sixth Region of Somalia," *Al Jazeera English*, September 5, 2011, available at http://www.aljazeera.com/news/africa/2011/09/201195104317598222.html; Camus,

Caligula and Three Other Plays, 134.

40. Franz Neumann, *Behemoth: The Structure and Practice of National Socialism, 1933–1944* (Oxford: Oxford University Press, 1944), 167.

41. Walter Benjamin, "On the Concept of History" (1940), available at http://www.marxists.org/reference/archive/benjamin/1940/history.htm.

42. Ulrike Meinhof, *Everybody Talks about the Weather . . . We Don't*, ed. Karin Bauer (New York: Seven Stories Press, 2008), 118.

43. Theodor W. Adorno, *Negative Dialectics*, trans. E. B. Ashton (London: Routledge, 1973), 218.

44. Chronis Polychroniou, "Interview with Professor Minqi Li," *Eleftherotypia* 13 (November 2009), available at http://www.econ.utah.edu/~mli/CV/Interview%20with%20Minqi%20Li_Greece%20111309.pdf.

45. Maurice Merleau-Ponty, *Humanism and Terror*, trans. John O'Neill (1947; repr., Boston: Beacon Press, 1969), 156; Theodor W. Adorno, "Progress," in *Benjamin: Philosophy, Aesthetics, History*, ed. Gary Smith (1962; repr., Chicago: University of Chicago Press, 1989), 85–86.

46. Walter Benjamin, *Illuminations*, ed. Hannah Arendt (New York: Harcourt, 1968), 38; Adorno, *Critical Models*, 190.

47. Adorno, *Negative Dialectics*, 405.

48. Samir Amin, "An Arab Springtime?" *Monthly Review*, June 2, 2011, available at http://monthlyreview.org/commentary/2011-an-arab-springtime; Immanuel Wallerstein, "The Contradictions of the Arab Spring," *Al Jazeera* English, November 14, 2011.

49. Karl Marx and Friedrich Engels, *The German Ideology, Part One*, ed. C. J. Arthur (New York: International Publishers, 2004), 57.

50. Adorno, *Critical Models*, 267–68.

51. Theodor W. Adorno, *Prisms*, trans. Samuel Weber and Shierry Weber (Cambridge, MA: MIT Press, 1967), 117.

52. Raoul Vaneigem, "Basic Banalities," in *Situationist International Anthology*, ed. Ken Knabb (Berkeley: Bureau of Public Secrets, 2006), 117–30.

53. Adorno, "Progress," in *Benjamin: Philosophy, Aesthetics, History*, ed. Gary Smith (1962; repr., Chicago: University of Chicago Press, 1989), 96.

54. Hannah Arendt, *The Human Condition* (Chicago: University of Chicago Press, 1958), 246.

The Death of Life?

1. Giorgio Agamben, *Remnants of Auschwitz: The Witness and the Archive*, trans. Daniel Heller-Roazen (New York: Zone Books, 2002), 121.

2. Noam Chomsky, *Hegemony or Survival: America's Quest for Global Dominance* (New York: Owl Books, 2004), 216.

3. Jonathan Schell, *The Fate of the Earth* (1982; repr., Stanford, CA: Stanford University Press, 2000), 21, 168.

4. Charles Fourier, *Design for Utopia: Selected Works of Charles Fourier* (New York: Schocken Books, 1971); Theodor W. Adorno, *Critical Models,* trans. Henry W. Pickford (New York: Columbia University Press, 2005), 273.

5. Schell, *The Fate of the Earth*, 115, xxvi, 118.

6. Ibid., 110, 148.

7. Ibid., 130–32, 95; Hannah Arendt, *The Promise of Politics*, ed. Jerome Kohn (New York: Schocken Books, 2005), 191; Günther Anders, "One World or No World," in *Hiroshima in Memoriam and Today: A Testament of Peace for the World*

(Asheville, NC: Biltmore Press, 1971), 210.

8. Schell, *The Abolition*, 46.

9. Schell, The *Fate of the Earth*, 178.

10. Ibid., 188.

11. P. D. James, *The Children of Men* (New York: Warner Books, 1992), 308.

12. Schell, *The Abolition*, 123; Schell, *The Fate of the Earth*, 110, 94, 186.

13. Schell, *The Fate of the Earth*, 148, 184.

14. Ibid., 161.

15. Ibid., 135, 226.

16. Ibid., 161, 135, 226, 177, 184, 173, 162, 188, 219, 122, 231, 223; Schell, *The Abolition*, 74.

17. Schell, *The Fate of the Earth*, 136, 173, 174, 177.

18. Ibid., 170, 225.

19. Ibid., 210, 218, 186, 219–31.

20. Bryan Farrell, "The Power of Nonviolent Movements," *Yes Magazine*, January 14, 2010.

21. Schell, *The Fate of the Earth*, 196, 169; Schell, *The Abolition*, 21.

22. Schell, *The Fate of the Earth*, 231; Schell, *The Abolition*, 11.

23. Walter Benjamin, *On Hashish*, ed. Howard Eiland (Cambridge, MA: Harvard University Press, 2006), 101.

24. Noam Chomsky, "Occupy the Future," *In These Times*, November 1, 2011.

25. James Hansen, *Storms of My Grandchildren* (New York: Bloomsbury, 2009), ix, 277.

26. David Spratt and Philip Sutton, *Climate Code Red: The Case for Emergency Action* (Melbourne: Scribe, 2008), 82.

27. Gwynne Dyer, *Climate Wars* (Toronto: Vintage Canada,

2009), 87–95; Mark Lynas, *Six Degrees: Our Future on a Hotter Planet* (Washington, DC: National Geographic, 2008), 274–75.

28. James Hansen, Makiko Sato, Pushker Kharecha, David Beerling, Valerie Masson-Delmotte, Mark Pagani, Maureen Raymo, Dana L. Royer, and James C. Zachos, "Target Atmospheric CO_2: Where Should Humanity Aim?" available at http://www.columbia.edu/~jeh1/2008/TargetCO2_20080407.pdf.

29. Spratt and Sutton, *Climate Code Red*, 120–32.

30. Steve Connor, "Extreme Weather Link 'Can No Longer Be Ignored,'" *Independent*, July 1, 2011.

31. *"Pakistan Floods in Numbers," Al Jazeera* English, August 30, 2010; Reena Saeed Khan, "The Floods in Pakistan Show Our Vulnerability to Climate Chaos," *Guardian*, November 10, 2010; Ali Ismail, "Pakistan Floods Unleash Desperate Economic Crisis," *World Socialist Web Site,* 26 August 26, 2010.

32. Declan Walsh, Shehryar Mufti, Lindsay Poulton, and Ziad Zafar, "Pakistan Floods: Feudals under Fire in Punjab," *Guardian*, October 3, 2010.

33. Tom Peters, "International Aid for Pakistan Flood Victims Grossly Inadequate," *World Socialist Web Site,* September 24, 2010.

34. Declan Walsh, "Pakistan Flood Crisis as Bad as African Famines, UN Says," *Guardian*, January 27, 2011.

35. "Millions Affected by Deadly Pakistan Floods," *Al Jazeera* English, September 9, 2011.

36. Rob Crilly, "Strong Evidence Climate Change Caused Devastating Pakistan Floods," *Scotsman News*, October 14, 2010.

37. Bill McKibben, "Why Has Extreme Weather Failed to Heat Up Climate Debate?" *Guardian*, August 18, 2010.

38. Mark Tran, "Global Response to Pakistan Floods Inadequate, Claims Report," *Guardian*, July 24, 2011.

39. "Niger's Silent Crisis," *BBC News Online*, June 21, 2010; Mike Pflanz, "Millions of West Africans Need Urgent Food Aid after Failed Harvests," *Telegraph,* June 21, 2010.

40. Henry Foy, "Millions Face Starvation in West Africa, Aid Agencies Warn," *Guardian*, June 21, 2010.

41. "Food Crisis Emergency in Niger," *ReliefWeb,* June 21, 2010.

42. Connor, "Extreme Weather"; Tom Parfitt, "Vladimir Putin Bans Grain Exports as Drought and Wildfires Ravage Crops," *Guardian*, August 5, 2010.

43. Katie Allen, "Afghanistan and African Nations at Greatest Risk from World Food Shortages," *Guardian*, August 19, 2010.

44. Jason Burke, "Hundreds Die in Indian Heat Wave," *Guardian*, May 30, 2010; John Vidal and Declan Walsh, "Temperatures Reach Record High in Pakistan," *Guardian*, June 1, 2010.

45. Karen McVeigh, "Sri Lankan Floods Could Leave 400,000 Children without Enough Food," *Guardian*, January 20, 2011; "Sri Lanka Floods Destroy Crops," *Al Jazeera* English, January 23, 2011.

46. Tom Phillips, "Drought Brings Amazon Tributary to Lowest Level in a Century," *Guardian*, October 26, 2010; Damian Carringon, "Mass Tree Death Prompts Fears of Amazon 'Climate Tipping Point,'" *Guardian*, February 3, 2011.

47. University of Colorado at Boulder, "Arctic Sea Ice Reaches Lowest 2010 Extent, Third Lowest in Satellite Record," *Science Daily*, September 16, 2010; Steve Connor, "Arctic Ice Set to Match All-time Record Low," *Independent*, September 7, 2011; Stephen Leahy, "Arctic Ice in Death Spiral," Inter Press Service,

September 20, 2010.

48. John Vidal, "Environment World Review of the Year: '2011 Rewrote the Record Books,'" *Guardian*, December 22, 2011; Fiona Harvey, "England Sees Driest Spring in a Century as Drought Hits UK," *Guardian*, June 10, 2011.

49. Jonathan Watts, "China Crisis over Yangtze River Drought Forces Drastic Dam Measures," *Guardian*, May 25, 2011.

50. David Randall, Simon Murphy, and Daud Yussuf, "Starvation Returns to the Horn of Africa," *Independent*, July 3, 2011.

51. Emily Dugan, "More Than Half of Somalis Now Face Starvation," *Independent*, September 4, 2011; Emily Dugan, "Two Million East African Infants Are Now Starving," *Independent*, August 7, 2011.

52. "Somalia Famine: UN Warns of 750,000 Deaths," *BBC News Online*, September 5, 2011.

53. Susan Solomon, Dahe Qin, Michael Manning, Zhenlin Chen, Melinda Marquis, Kristen B. Averyt, Melinda Tignor, and Henry L. Miller, *Contribution of Working Group I to the Fourth Assessment Report of the Intergovernmental Panel on Climate Change* (Cambridge: Cambridge University Press, 2007), 310–12.

54. Collectif Argos, *Climate Refugees* (Cambridge, MA: MIT Press, 2010), 273; Priestley Habru, "The View from beneath the Waves: Climate Change in the Solomon Islands," *Guardian*, November 9, 2010.

55. Kathy Marks, "Sinking Pacific Island Kiribati Considers Moving to a Man-made Alternative," *Independent*, September 8, 2011; Kit Gillet, "Vietnam's Rice Bowl Threatened by Rising

Seas," *Guardian*, August 21, 2011.

56. Collectif Argos, *Climate Refugees*, 93; Daniel Howden, "Record Heat Recorded for Africa's Greatest Lake," *Independent*, 18 May 18, 2010.

57. Robin McKie, "Ocean Acidification Is Latest Manifestation of Global Warming," *Observer*, May 29, 2011.

58. Jayashree Nandi, "Isro: 75% of Himalayan Glaciers Retreating," *Times of India*, May 16, 2011.

59. Jonathan Watts, "Tibet Temperature 'Highest since Records Began' Say Chinese Climatologists," *Guardian*, February 2, 2010.

60. Nikolas Kozloff, *No Rain in the Amazon* (New York: Palgrave Macmillan, 2010), 9.

61. Steve Connor, "Weather Disasters in the Poorest Nations 'Have Trebled since 1980s,'" *Independent*, May 23, 2011.

62. Edward S. Herman and David Peterson, *The Politics of Genocide* (New York: Monthly Review Press, 2010), 42.

63. Michael McCarthy, "Revealed: Climate Quirk That Doubles Risk of War," *Independent*, August 25, 2011.

64. Mike Davis, *Late Victorian Holocausts: El Niño Famines and the Making of the Third World* (London: Verso, 2000), 7.

65. Solomon, Qin, Manning, Chen, Marquis, Averyt, Tignor, and Miller, *Contribution of Working Group I*, 790.

66. James Hansen, Pushker Kharecha, Makiko Sato, Paul Epstein, Paul J. Hearty, Ove Hoegh-Guldberg, Camille Parmesan, Stefan Rahmstorf, Johan Rockstrom, Eelco J. Rohling, Jeffrey Sachs, Peter Smith, Konrad Steffen, Karina von Schuckmann, and James C. Zachos, "The Case for Young People and Nature: A Path to a Healthy, Natural, Prosperous Future," available at http://www.columbia.edu/~jeh1/

mailings/2011/20110505_CaseForYoungPeople.pdf.

67. Lynas, *Six Degrees*, 25–70, 73–119.

68. Simon Hales, "Estimating Human Population Health Impacts in a 4+°C World" (paper presented at the Oxford University 4 Degrees and Beyond International Climate Change Conference, Oxford, September 28, 2009).

69. Dyer, *Climate Wars*, 62.

70. Lynas, *Six Degrees*, 123–81.

71. Hans Joachim Schellnhuber, "Terra Quasi-Incognita: Beyond the 2°C Line" (paper presented at the Oxford University 4 Degrees and Beyond International Climate Change Conference, Oxford, September 28, 2009).

72. Peter D. Ward, *The Flooded Earth: Our Future in a World Without Ice Caps* (New York: Basic Books, 2010).

73. Steve Connor, "Melting of the Arctic 'Will Accelerate Climate Change within Twenty Years,'" *Independent*, May 30, 2011.

74. AFP, "Russia May Lose 30% of Permafrost by 2050: Official," *Independent*, July 31, 2011.

75. David Chandler, "Climate Change Odds Much Worse Than Thought," MIT News Office, May 19, 2009.

76. Dyer, *Climate Wars*, 90.

77. Jane B. Reece, Lisa A. Urry, Michael L. Cain, Steven A. Wasserman, Peter V. Minorsky, and Robert B. Jackson, *Campbell Biology* (Boston: Benjamin Cummings, 2011), 521–23.

78. Hansen, *Storms of My Grandchildren*, 223–36.

Fragmentary Critique

1. Herbert Marcuse, *Counterrevolution and Revolt* (Boston: Beacon Press, 1972), 60.

2. Theodor W. Adorno, *Aesthetic Theory*, trans. Robert

Hullot-Kentor (1970; repr., London: Continuum, 2002), 66.

3. Theodor W. Adorno, *History and Freedom*, trans. Rodney Livingstone (1964–65; repr., London: Polity Press, 2006), 45; Max Horkheimer and Theodor W. Adorno, *Dialectic of Enlightenment: Philosophical Fragments*, trans. Edmund Jephcott (1947; repr., Stanford, CA: Stanford University Press, 2002), 165.

4. Steven Best, "Minding the Animals: Ethology and the Obsolescence of Left Humanism," *International Journal of Inclusive Democracy* 5, no. 2 (Spring 2009), available at http://www.inclusivedemocracy.org/journal/vol5/vol5_no2_best_minding_animals_PRINTABLE.htm.

5. Christopher Boehm, *Hierarchy in the Forest: The Evolution of Egalitarian Behavior* (Cambridge, MA: Harvard University Press, 2001).

6. Cited in Murray Bookchin, *The Ecology of Freedom* (1982; repr., Oakland, CA: AK Press, 2005), 93.

7. Friedrich Engels, *The Origin of the Family, Private Property, and the State* (1891; repr., New York: Pathfinder, 1972), 54.

8. Herbert Marcuse, *Eros and Civilization: A Philosophical Inquiry into Freud* (Boston: Beacon Press, 1966), 109.

9. Horkheimer and Adorno, *Dialectic of Enlightenment*, 212.

10. Theodor W. Adorno, *Negative Dialectics*, trans. E. B. Ashton (London: Routledge, 1973), 355.

11. Peter Kropotkin, *Mutual Aid: A Factor of Evolution* (1902; repr., Westford, MA: Porter Sargent, 1976).

12. Collectif Argos, *Climate Refugees* (Cambridge, MA: MIT Press, 2010), 9, 14.

13. Ibid., 28, 60, 97.

14. James D. Cockcroft, *Mexico's Revolution Then and Now* (New York: Monthly Review Press, 2010), 141.

15. Adorno, *Negative Dialectics*, 377–78.

16. John Bellamy Foster, *Marx's Ecology* (New York: Monthly Review, 2000); John Bellamy Foster, *The Ecological Revolution* (New York: Monthly Review, 2009).

17. Cited in *Karl Marx and Frederick Engels: Collected Works* (Moscow: International Publishers, 1975), 12:132; Karl Marx, *Economic and Philosophical Manuscripts of 1844*, trans. Martin Milligan, ed. Dirk J. Struik (New York: International Publishers), 112.

18. Rosa Luxemburg, *The Rosa Luxemburg Reader*, ed. Peter Hudis and Kevin B. Anderson (New York: Monthly Review Press, 2004), 394, 390–91.

19. Ernst Bloch, *The Principle of Hope*, trans. Neville Plaice, Stephen Plaice, and Paul Knight (1959; repr., Cambridge, MA: MIT Press, 1986), 286.

20. Adorno, *Aesthetic Theory*, 65.

21. Bill McKibben, *Eaarth: Making a Life on a Tough New Planet* (New York: Times Books, 2010), 101, 78, 52.

22. Ibid., 27.

23. Noam Chomsky, "Crisis and Hope: Theirs and Ours" (comments at the Brecht Forum, Riverside Church, New York, June 12, 2009).

24. McKibben, *Eaarth*, 35.

25. Ibid., 52.

26. Walter Benjamin, *Selected Writings, Volume 4: 1938–1940*, trans. Edmund Jephcott, ed. Howard Eiland and Michael W. Jennings (Cambridge, MA: Harvard University Press, 2003), 402.

27. Marcuse, *Counterrevolution and Revolt*, 64.

28. Ibid., 65, 69.

29. Ibid., 67; Marcuse, *Eros and Civilization*, 178.

30. Marcuse, *Counterrevolution and Revolt*, 164, 178.

31. Leo Hickman, "James Lovelock: Humans Are Too Stupid to Prevent Climate Change" and "James Lovelock on the Value of Sceptics and Why Copenhagen Was Doomed," *Guardian*, March 29, 2010; see also Micah White, "An Alternative to the New Wave of Ecofascism," *Guardian*, September 16, 2010.

32. Susanna Rustin, "Has the Green Movement Lost Its Way?" *Guardian,* July 1, 2011.

On Hope and Reason Today

1. James C. Scott, *The Art of Not Being Governed* (New Haven, CT: Yale University Press, 2009), 293.

2. Ernst Bloch, *The Principle of Hope*, trans. Neville Plaice, Stephen Plaice, and Paul Knight (1959; repr., Cambridge, MA: MIT Press, 1986), 189.

3. Michael Hardt and Antonio Negri, *Commonwealth* (Cambridge, MA: Harvard University Press, 2009), 198.

4. Theodor W. Adorno, *Negative Dialectics*, trans. E. B. Ashton (London: Routledge, 1973), 398; Hannah Arendt, *Responsibility and Judgment*, ed. Jerome Kohn (New York: Schocken Books, 2003), 164.

5. Theodor W. Adorno, *Critical Models*, trans. Henry W. Pickford (New York: Columbia University Press, 2005), 272–73.

6. Hannah Arendt, *On Violence* (San Diego: Harcourt, 1969), 48.

7. Theodor W. Adorno, *Can One Live After Auschwitz? A Philosophical Reader* (Stanford, CA: Stanford University Press, 2003), 18.

8. Noam Chomsky, *Hopes and Prospects* (Chicago:

Haymarket Books, 2010), 165.

9. Noam Chomsky, *Hegemony or Survival: America's Quest for Global Dominance* (New York: Owl Books, 2004), 1–2; Chomsky, *Hopes and Prospects*, 175.

10. Mark Achbar and Peter Wintonick, *Manufacturing Consent: Noam Chomsky and the Media* (Montreal: Necessary Illusions/National Film Board of Canada, 1992); Noam Chomsky, "Crisis and Hope: Theirs and Ours" (comments at the Brecht Forum, Riverside Church, New York, June 12, 2009).

11. Chomsky, *Hegemony or Survival*, 218, 222.

12. Ibid., 225–27.

13. Ibid., 228.

14. Ibid., 228; Chomsky, *Hopes and Prospects*, 85.

15. Bill Van Auken, "Obama Administration Spending Billions on New Global Strike Weapons," World Socialist Web Site, April 24, 2010; Alok Jha, "US Military to Launch Fastest-Ever Plane," *Guardian*, August 10, 2011, available at http://www.guardian.co.uk/world/2011/aug/10/us-military-fastest-plane-falcon.

16. Chomsky, *Hegemony or Survival*, 229.

17. Chomsky, *Hopes and Prospects*, 27, 108.

18. Noam Chomsky, "Human Intelligence and the Environment," *International Socialist Review* 76 (May 2011), 45.

19. Chomsky, *Hopes and Prospects*, 111–12.

20. Chomsky, *Hegemony or Survival*, 234–35.

21. Chomsky, *Hopes and Prospects*, 112.

22. Chomsky, *Hegemony or Survival*, 235.

23. Ibid., 36; Chomsky, *Hopes and Prospects*, 4–7.

24. Chomsky, *Hegemony or Survival*, 97; Chomsky, *Hopes and Prospects*, 37.

25. Chomsky, *Hopes and Prospects*, 55, 116; Noam Chomsky, *New World of Indigenous Resistance*, ed. Lois Meyer and Benjamín Maldonado Alvarado (San Francisco: City Lights Books, 2010), 53.

26. Nick Nesbitt, *Universal Emancipation: The Haitian Revolution and the Radical Enlightenment* (Charlottesville: University of Virginia Press, 2008), 195.

27. Scott, *The Art of Not Being Governed*; Hannah Arendt, *On Revolution* (1963; repr., New York: Penguin, 2006), 237, 256–58.

28. Chomsky, *Hopes and Prospects*, 38.

29. Ibid., 228; Chomsky, *Hegemony or Survival*, 29.

30. Chomsky, *Hegemony or Survival*, 38; Chomsky, *Hopes and Prospects*, 121.

31. Jacques Rancière, *Disagreement: Politics and Philosophy*, trans. Julie Rose (Minneapolis: University of Minnesota Press, 1999).

32. Chomsky, *Hopes and Prospects*, 112, 215.

33. Chomsky, *Hegemony or Survival*, 182; Chomsky, *Hopes and Prospects*, 156.

34. Chomsky, *Hegemony or Survival*, 216.

35. Wilhelm Reich, *The Mass Psychology of Fascism* (New York: Farrar, Straus and Giroux, 1970), xxxi. On autonomous Marxism, see Antonio Negri, *Marx Beyond Marx: Lessons on the Grundrisse*, trans. Harry Cleaver (South Hadley, MA: Bergin and Garvey Publishers, 1984); John Holloway, *Crack Capitalism* (London: Pluto Press, 2010); Chomsky, *Hopes and Prospects*, 167.

36. Chomsky, *Hopes and Prospects*, 118.

37. Noam Chomsky, "All Students Should Become Anarchists," June 14, 2011, available at http://www.chomsky.info/interviews/20110614_en.htm; Chomsky, *New World of*

Indigenous Resistance, 361.

38. Chomsky, *Hopes and Prospects*, 135–36.

39. Fidel Castro, "El Invierno Nuclear" *La Jornada*, August 23, 2010.

40. Chomsky, *Hopes and Prospects*, 135–36.

41. Ibid., 166; Chomsky,, "Human Intelligence and the Environment," 49.

42. Chomsky, "Human Intelligence and the Environment," 51.

43. Theodor W. Adorno, *Problems of Moral Philosophy*, trans. Rodney Livingstone (1963; repr., Stanford, CA: Stanford University Press, 2001), 14; Theodor W. Adorno, *Minima Moralia: Reflections on a Damaged Life*, trans. E.F.N. Jephcott (1951; repr., London: Verso, 1974), 39 (translation modified); Theodor W. Adorno, "Progress," in *Benjamin: Philosophy, Aesthetics, History*, ed. Gary Smith (1962; repr., Chicago: University of Chicago Press, 1989), 84–85.

44. Theodor W. Adorno, *History and Freedom*, trans. Rodney Livingstone (1964–65; repr., London: Polity Press, 2006), 4.

45. Ibid., 47, 8; Adorno, *Problems of Moral Philosophy*, 10.

46. Adorno, *Can One Live After Auschwitz?* 244, 13.

47. Theodor W. Adorno, *Prisms*, trans. Samuel Weber and Shierry Weber (Cambridge, MA: MIT Press, 1967), 257.

48. Adorno, *Problems of Moral Philosophy*, 99, 167.

49. Theodor W. Adorno and Max Horkheimer, *Towards a New Manifesto?* trans. Rodney Livingstone (1989; repr., London: Verso, 2011), 37.

50. Adorno, "Progress," 84 (translation modified).

51. Adorno and Horkheimer, *Towards a New Manifesto?* 40.

52. Adorno, *History and Freedom*, 143.

53. Adorno, "Progress," 85.

54. Adorno, *History and Freedom*, 145.

55. Mikhail Bakunin, "Man, Society, and Freedom," from *Bakunin on Anarchy*, trans. Sam Dolgoff (New York: Knopf, 1972), 237 and Adorno, *Minima Moralia*, 173.

56. Simone de Beauvoir, *Ethics of Ambiguity*, trans. Bernard Frechtman (New York: Philosophical Library, 1948), 91.

57. Adorno, "Progress," 85.

58. Adorno and Horkheimer, *Towards a New Manifesto?* 48.

59. Hannah Arendt, *The Origins of Totalitarianism* (1951; repr., San Diego, CA: Harcourt, 1968), xx; Adorno, "Progress," 94.

60. Walter Benjamin, "On the Concept of History" (1940), available at http://www.marxists.org/reference/archive/benjamin/1940/history.htm; Adorno, "Progress," 36.

61. Adorno, *History and Freedom*, 181.

62. Murray Bookchin, *Post-Scarcity Anarchism* (Oakland, CA: AK Press, 2004).

63. Adorno, *History and Freedom*, 62, 182.

64. Adorno, "Progress," 94.

65. Adorno and Horkheimer, *Towards a New Manifesto?* 47; Adorno, *History and Freedom*, 111.

66. Adorno, "Progress," 99–101.

67. Adorno, *History and Freedom*, 150; Adorno, *Problems of Moral Philosophy*, 103.

68. Adorno and Horkheimer, *Towards a New Manifesto?*, 52.

69. Adorno, "Progress," 85 (translation modified).

70. Ibid., 90–91.

71. Ibid., 96.

72. Horkheimer and Adorno, *Dialectic of Enlightenment*, 100, x, 194.

73. Adorno, *Negative Dialectics*, 404.

74. Theodor W. Adorno, *The Culture Industry* (London: Routledge, 1991), 196.

75. Adorno, *Critical Models*, 269; Theodor W. Adorno, *Guilt and Defense: On the Legacies of National Socialism in Postwar Germany*, trans. and ed. Jeffrey K. Olick and Andrew J. Perrin (Cambridge, MA: Harvard University Press, 2010), 169–84.

76. Adorno and Horkheimer, *Towards a New Manifesto?* 36.

77. Max Horkheimer, "The End of Reason," in *The Essential Frankfurt School Reader*, ed. Andrew Arato and Eike Gebhardt (New York: Continuum, 1997), 48.

78. Adorno and Horkheimer, *Towards a New Manifesto?* 43; Adorno, *Negative Dialectics*, 320.

79. Adorno and Horkheimer, *Towards a New Manifesto?* 47.

80. Adorno, *Critical Models*, 150 (translation modified).

81. Robert L. Heilbroner, *An Inquiry into the Human Prospect* (New York: W. W. Norton, 1980).

82. Ibid., 43.

83. Ibid., 22, 42–46, 97.

84. Ibid., 50–55, 150, 109.

85. Ibid., 93, 91.

86. Ibid., 57, 77, 93, 91, 94, 98–104, 109, 153, 109.

87. Ibid., 130–35.

88. Ibid., 157, 110, 155, 130–35, 165.

89. Max Horkheimer, *Dawn and Decline: Notes, 1926–1931 and 1959–1969*, trans. Michael Shaw (New York: Seabury Press, 1978), 202.

90. Heilbroner, *Inquiry*, 165–66, 184.

91. Ronald Aronson, *Dialectics of Disaster: A Preface to Hope* (New York: Schocken Books, 1984), 3, 191.

92. Ibid., 35–45, 77, 142, 169, 262.

93. Ibid., 262, 266, 286, 288, 303.

94. Ibid., 302, 292, 210, 17, 304, 289.

95. Fidel Castro, "La Paz con la Paz Se Paga," September 3, 2010, available at http://www.cubadebate.cu/noticias/2010/09/03/fidel-castro-la-paz-con-la-paz-se-paga.

96. Rancière, *Disagreement*, 83.

97. McKibben, *Eaarth*, xv.

98. Heilbroner, *Inquiry*, 159.

99. Bloch, *Principle of Hope*, 232.

100. Chomsky, *New World of Indigenous Resistance*, 362.

101. Cornelius Castoriadis, *The Castoriadis Reader*, trans. and ed. David Ames Curtis (Oxford: Blackwell, 1997), 107.

102. Adorno and Horkheimer, *Towards a New Manifesto?*, 45, 39, 61.

103. Franz Neumann, *Behemoth: The Structure and Practice of National Socialism, 1933–1944* (Oxford: Oxford University Press, 1944), 464.

104. Adorno and Horkheimer, *Towards a New Manifesto?*, 42.

105. Chomsky, *Hopes and Prospects*, 195; Bill Van Auken, "Obama Administration Spending Billions on New Global Strike Weapons," World Socialist Web Site, April 24, 2010.

106. George Monbiot, "The Western Appetite for Biofuels Is Causing Starvation in the Poor World," *Guardian*, November 6, 2007.

107. Adorno and Horkheimer, *Towards a New Manifesto?* 45; Gareth Porter, "Report Slams Pakistan Drone Attacks," *Al Jazeera* English, November 3, 2010.

108. Bloch, *The Principle of Hope*; Holloway, *Crack Capitalism*.

109. Adorno, *History and Freedom*, 149; David Harvey, *The*

Enigma of Capital (Oxford: Oxford University Press, 2009), 226–27.

110. Adorno, *History and Freedom*, 7.

111. Arendt, *Origins of Totalitarianism*, 437.

112. Max Horkheimer, *Eclipse of Reason* (1947; repr., London: Continuum, 2004), 115; Henry A. Giroux, "In the Twilight of the Social State: Rethinking Walter Benjamin's Angel of History," *Truth-out*, January 4, 2011, available at http://www.truth-out.org/in-twilight-social-state-rethinking-walter-benjamins-angel-history66544.

113. Walter Benjamin, *Benjamin: Philosophy, Aesthetics, History*, ed. Gary Smith (1962; repr., Chicago: University of Chicago Press, 1989), 64.

114. Chris Hedges, "Zero Point of Systemic Collapse," *Adbusters*, February 8, 2010.

115. Benjamin, *Benjamin*, 66.

116. Adorno, *Problems of Moral Philosophy*, 176.

117. Rancière, *Disagreement*, 14; Adorno and Horkheimer, *Towards a New Manifesto?*, 36.

118. Horkheimer, "The Authoritarian State," in *The Essential Frankfurt School Reader*, ed. Andrew Arato and Eike Gebhardt (New York: Continuum, 1997), 117.

119. Holloway, *Crack Capitalism*, 192.

120. Ibid., 79; Marcuse, *One-Dimensional Man*, 257.

121. Hannah Arendt, *The Human Condition* (Chicago: University of Chicago Press, 1958), 247; de Beauvoir, *Ethics of Ambiguity*, 91.

On Adorno's New Categorical Imperative

1. Theodor W. Adorno, *Negative Dialectics*, trans. E. B.

Ashton (London: Routledge, 1973), 365.

2. Franciszek Piper, "The Number of Victims," in *Anatomy of the Auschwitz Death Camp*, ed. Yehuda Bauer, Raul Hilberg, and Franciszek Piper (Bloomington: Indiana University Press, 1994), 61–62.

3. Daniel Jonah Goldhagen, *Hitler's Willing Executioners: Ordinary Germans and the Holocaust* (New York: Vintage, 1996), 157; J. M. Bernstein, *Adorno: Disenchantment and Ethics* (Cambridge: Cambridge University Press, 2001), 409.

4. Theodor W. Adorno, *Critical Models*, trans. Henry W. Pickford (New York: Columbia University Press, 2005), 191.

5. Karl Jaspers, *Kant*, ed. Hannah Arendt, trans. Ralph Manheim (San Diego: Harcourt, 1962), 65.

6. Adorno, *Critical Models*, 191.

7. Adorno, *Negative Dialectics*, 365.

8. Bernstein, *Adorno*, 387; quoted in Peter M. R. Stirk, *Max Horkheimer: A New Interpretation* (Hertfordshire, UK: Harvester Wheatsheaf, 1992), 190.

9. Theodor W. Adorno and Max Horkheimer, *Dialectic of Enlightenment: Philosophical Fragments*, trans. Edmund Jephcott (1947; repr., Stanford, CA: Stanford University Press, 2002), 165; Adorno, *Minima Moralia*, 240.

10. Emmanuel Levinas, *Otherwise Than Being, or Beyond Essence*, trans. Alphonso Lingis (Pittsburgh: Duquesne University Press, 1998).

11. Bernstein, *Disenchantment and Ethics*, 382.

12. Bernstein, *Adorno*, 382, 394.

13. Edmund Stillman and William Pfaff, *The Politics of Hysteria* (New York: Harper and Row, 1964), 30–31.

14. Zygmunt Bauman, *Modernity and the Holocaust* (Ithaca,

NY: Cornell University Press, 1989), 17.

15. Ibid., 384; Adorno, *Negative Dialectics*, 362; Max Weber, *From Max Weber: Essays in Sociology*, ed. H. H. Gerth and C. Wright Mills (London: Routledge and Kegan Paul, 1970), 214–15.

16. Adorno, *Negative Dialectics*, 362.

17. Adorno, *Critical Models*, 305.

18. Bauman, *Modernity and the Holocaust*, xiii.

19. Rosa Luxemburg, *The Rosa Luxemburg Reader*, ed. Peter Hudis and Kevin B. Anderson (New York: Monthly Review Press, 2004), 242–45; Hannah Arendt, *Origins of Totalitarianism* (1951; repr., San Diego, CA: Harcourt, 1968), 206.

20. Pierre Clastres, *Society against the State* (1974; repr., New York: Zone Books: 1989), 99.

21. Aimé Césaire, *Discourse on Colonialism*, trans. Joan Pinkham (1955; repr., New York: Monthly Review Press, 2001), 36–37.

22. Luxemburg, *The Rosa Luxemburg Reader*, 244–45; Mike Davis, *Late Victorian Holocausts: El Niño Famines and the Making of the Third World* (London: Verso, 2000).

23. Fredric Jameson, *Late Marxism: Adorno, or the Persistence of the Dialectic* (London: Verso, 1990), 4–5, 7.

24. Gilbert Achcar, *The Arabs and the Holocaust*, trans. G. M. Goshgarian (New York: Metropolitan, 2009), 132.

25. Adorno, *Critical Models*, 192, 268.

26. Theodor W. Adorno and Herbert Marcuse, "Correspondence on the German Student Movement," *New Left Review* 1, no. 233 (January–February 1999): 127.

27. Theodor W. Adorno, *Metaphysics: Concepts and Problems*, trans. Edmund Jephcott, ed. Rolf Tiedemann (1965; repr., Stanford, CA: Stanford University Press, 2000), 101.

28. Claude Eatherly and Günther Anders, *Burning Conscience*

(New York: Monthly Review Press, 1962), 5.

29. Franz Neumann, *Behemoth: The Structure and Practice of National Socialism, 1933–1944* (Oxford: Oxford University Press, 1944), 202.

30. Goldhagen, *Hitler's Willing Executioners*, 59, 63.

31. Norman G. Finkelstein and Ruth Bettina Birn, *A Nation on Trial: The Goldhagen Thesis and Historical Truth* (New York: Henry Holt, 1998), 18–46.

32. Bauman, *Modernity and the Holocaust*, 73–74, 31, 78–79, 107–10.

33. Nicolas Holliman, "Notes from the Steam Room: On the Origins of Industrialised Killing during WWII," *Principia Dialectica*, September 9, 2011.

34. Richard A. Koenigsberg, *Nations Have the Right to Kill* (New York: Library of Social Science, 2009).

35. Adorno, *Critical Models*, 203; Hannah Arendt, *Eichmann in Jerusalem: A Report on the Banality of Evil* (1963; repr., New York: Penguin, 2006), 21.

36. Wilhelm Reich, *The Mass Psychology of Fascism* (New York: Farrar, Straus and Giroux, 1970), 48–67, 104–14.

37. Adorno, *Critical Models*, 201.

38. Arendt, *Eichmann in Jerusalem*, 98; Ingrid Strobl, *Partisanas* (1989; repr., Oakland, CA: AK Press, 2008).

39. Jacques Derrida, *Specters of Marx: The State of Debt, the Work of Mourning, and the New International*, trans. Peggy Kamuf (New York: Routledge, 1994), 106.

40. Theodor W. Adorno and Max Horkheimer, *Towards a New Manifesto?*, trans. Rodney Livingstone (1989; repr., London: Verso, 2011), 47.

41. Adorno, *Critical Models*, 192.

42. Bill McKibben, *Eaarth: Making a Life on a Tough New Planet* (New York: Times Books, 2010), 25.

43. Maia Ramnath, introduction to *Perspectives on Anarchist Theory* 12, no. 2 (Fall 2010): 4.

44. Jean Améry, *At the Mind's Limits: Contemplations by a Survivor on Auschwitz and Its Realities*, trans. Sidney Rosenfeld and Stella P. Rosenfeld (Bloomington: Indiana University Press, 1980), 9; Giorgio Agamben, *Remnants of Auschwitz: The Witness and the Archive*, trans. Daniel Heller-Roazen (New York: Zone Books, 2002), 41–86, 166–71.

45. Wolfgang Sofsky, quoted in Bernstein, *Adorno*, 373.

46. "U.S. Vows Sharp CO_2 Cuts, But Will Not Pay Climate 'Reparations,'" *Yale Environment 360*, December 9, 2009; quoted in Arendt, *Eichmann in Jerusalem*, 24.

47. Quoted in Simon McGee, "Anger at Delegate's Holocaust Jibe against Climate Deal—as His Country Shares £62bn Bonanza [*sic*]," *Daily Mail*, December 20, 2009.

48. Adorno and Horkheimer, *Dialectic of Enlightenment*, 43.

49. Noam Chomsky, *Profit over People: Neoliberalism and Global Order* (New York: Seven Stories Press, 1999).

50. Hannah Arendt, *The Promise of Politics*, ed. Jerome Kohn (New York: Schocken Books, 2005), 120.

51. Noam Chomsky and Ilan Pappé, *Gaza in Crisis: Reflections on Israel's War against the Palestinians* (Chicago: Haymarket Books, 2010), 101.

52. See, for example, Gideon Polya, "G8 Failure Means Climate Genocide for Developing World," *Countercurrents*, July 11, 2009; see also http://sites.google.com/site/climategenocide/home; quoted in Gwynne Dyer, *Climate Wars* (Toronto: Vintage Canada, 2009), 59.

53. Violeta Davoliute and Ugur Ümit Üngör, "Genocides?" *Eurozine*, July 7, 2011.

54. Noam Chomsky, "'The Evil Scourge of Terrorism': Reality, Construction, Remedy" (comments at the International Erich Fromm Society, Stuttgart, March 23, 2010).

55. Quoted in Ronald Aronson, *Dialectics of Disaster: A Preface to Hope* (New York: Schocken Books, 1984), 164. The International War Crimes Tribunal was orgnized by Bertrand Russell and hosted by Sartre.

56. Giorgio Agamben, *The Coming Community*, trans. Michael Hardt (Minneapolis: University of Minnesota Press, 1993), 65.

57. Damian Carrington, "Climate Change Concern Tumbles in US and China," *Guardian*, August 30, 2011; Suzanne Goldenberg, "Most Americans Don't Believe Humans Responsible for Climate Change, Study Finds," *Guardian*, July 9, 2009; Suzanne Goldenberg, "Number of Americans Who Believe in Climate Change Drops, Survey Shows," *Guardian*, October 22, 2009.

58. Chris Hedges, *Empire of Illusion* (New York: Nation Books, 2009), 73.

59. Adorno and Horkheimer, *Dialectic of Enlightenment*, 167.

60. Cornelius Castoriadis, *The Castoriadis Reader*, trans. and ed. David Ames Curtis (Oxford: Blackwell, 1997), 311, 340; Marcuse, *Negations*, 14.

61. Bauman, *Modernity and the Holocaust*, 24.

62. David Orr, *Down to the Wire: Confronting Climate Collapse* (Oxford: Oxford University Press, 2009), 9.

63. Adorno, *Negative Dialectics*, 404; Herbert Marcuse, *The Aesthetic Dimension: Toward a Critique of Marxist Aesthetics* (Boston: Beacon Press, 1978), 73.

64. Michael Hardt and Antonio Negri, *Commonwealth* (Cambridge, MA: Harvard University Press, 2009), 212.

65. Max Horkheimer, *Between Philosophy and Social Science: Selected Early Writings*, trans. G. Frederick Hunter, Matthew S. Kramer, and John Torpey (Cambridge, MA: MIT Press, 1993), 25.

66. Bauman, *Modernity and the Holocaust*, 74–76.

67. Albert Camus, *The Rebel*, trans. Anthony Bower (New York: Alfred Knopf, 1956), 22.

68. Neumann, *Behemoth*, 476.

69. Michael Hardt and Antonio Negri, *Empire* (Cambridge, MA: Harvard University Press, 2001), 123.

70. Immanuel Kant, *Perpetual Peace*, ed. Leslie White Beck (1795; repr., Upper Saddle River, NJ: Prentice Hall, 1957), appendix 1.

71. Albert Memmi, *The Colonizer and the Colonized* (Boston: Beach Press, 1965), 128.

72. Arendt, *Eichmann in Jerusalem*, 233.

73. Bernstein, *Adorno*, 407.

74. Dyer, *Climate Wars*, 46.

75. Reich, *The Mass Psychology of Fascism*, 326, 345, 282, 216, 32 (emphasis in original).

76. Hannah Arendt, *Responsibility and Judgment*, ed. Jerome Kohn (New York: Schocken Books, 2003), 147, 164, 180.

77. Arendt, *Eichmann in Jerusalem*, 279.

78. Arendt, *The Promise of Politics*, 99, 120, 43.

79. Arendt, *Responsibility and Judgment*, 189.

80. Adorno, *Critical Models*, 195.

81. John Holloway, *Crack Capitalism* (London: Pluto Press, 2010), 169.

82. Max Horkheimer, *Dawn and Decline: Notes, 1926–1931*

and 1959–1969, trans. Michael Shaw (New York: Seabury Press, 1978), 39.

83. Maurice Merleau-Ponty, *Humanism and Terror*, trans. John O'Neill (1947; repr., Boston: Beacon Press, 1969), 129.

For an Ecological Anarcho-Communism

1. Herbert Marcuse, *Negations: Essays in Critical Theory*, trans. Jeremy J. Shapiro (Boston: Beacon Press, 1968), 156.

2. Yevgeny Zamyatin, *We*, trans. Clarence Brown (1924; repr., New York: Penguin, 1993), 168.

3. Bertolt Brecht, *The Days of the Commune*, trans. Clive Barker and Arno Reinfrank (1955; repr., London: Methuen, 1978), 72.

4. Walter Benjamin, *Benjamin: Philosophy, Aesthetics, History*, ed. Gary Smith (1962; repr., Chicago: University of Chicago Press, 1989), 66; Cornelius Castoriadis, *The Rising Tide of Insignificancy (The Big Sleep)*, 13, available at http://www.not-bored.org/RTI.pdf.

5. Noam Chomsky and Michel Foucault, *The Chomsky-Foucault Debate: On Human Nature* (New York: New Press, 2006), 50.

6. Theodor W. Adorno, *History and Freedom*, trans. Rodney Livingstone (1964–65; repr., London: Polity Press, 2006), 149; Cornelius Castoriadis, *The Castoriadis Reader*, trans. and ed. David Ames Curtis (Oxford: Blackwell, 1997), 241.

7. David Harvey, *Enigma of Capital* (Oxford: Oxford University Press, 2009), 227; David Harvey, *Spaces of Hope* (Berkeley: University of California Press, 2000), 260–63.

8. Takis Fotopoulos, "Direct Democracy and De-Growth," *International Journal of Inclusive Democracy* 6, no. 4 (Fall 2010).

9. Theodor W. Adorno, *Minima Moralia: Reflections on a Damaged Life*, trans. E.F.N. Jephcott (1951; repr., London: Verso, 1974), 156, 103 (translation modified).

10. Arthur Schopenhauer, *Suffering, Suicide, and Immortality: Eight Essays from the Parerga*, trans. T. Bailey Saunders (Mineola, NY: Dover, 2006), 16–17.

11. Jean-Jacques Rousseau, "Discourse on the Origin and Foundations of Inequality among Men," in *Modern Political Thought: Readings from Machiavelli to Nietzsche*, ed. David Wootton (1755; repr., Indianapolis: Hackett, 1996), 426.

12. Noam Chomsky, *Hegemony or Survival: America's Quest for Global Dominance* (New York: Owl Books, 2004), 236.

13. Renfrey Clark, "The 350 ppm Carbon Dioxide Challenge and How to Achieve It," *Links: International Journal of Socialist Renewal*, January 14, 2010.

14. Poorva Joshipura, "This Earth Day, Go Vegan," *Guardian*, April 22, 2010.

15. Herbert Marcuse, *Counterrevolution and Revolt* (Boston: Beacon Press, 1972), 265.

16. Herbert Marcuse, *Eros and Civilization: A Philosophical Inquiry into Freud* (Boston: Beacon Press, 1966), 5.

17. Brian Tokar, "Movements for Climate Action: Toward Utopia or Apocalypse?" in *Perspectives on Anarchist Theory* 12, no. 2 (Fall 2010): 65.

18. James Hansen, *Storms of My Grandchildren* (New York: Bloomsbury, 2009), 172–222.

19. Minqi Li, *The Rise of China and the Demise of the Capitalist World Economy* (New York: Monthly Review, 2008), 171–73.

20. Hans Joachim Schellnhuber, "Terra Quasi-Incognita: Beyond the 2°C Line" (paper presented at the Oxford

University 4 Degrees and Beyond International Climate Change Conference, Oxford, September 28, 2009); Ted Trainer, *Renewable Energy Cannot Sustain a Consumer Society* (Dordrecht, Netherlands: Springer, 2007), 126.

21. Peter D. Schwartzman and David D. Schwartzman, *A Solar Transition Is Possible* (London: Institute for Policy Research and Development, 2011).

22. Lester Brown, *World on the Edge: How to Prevent Environmental and Economic Collapse* (New York: W. W. Norton, 2011), 116–35.

23. Mark Jacobson and Mark Delucchi, "A Plan to Power 100 Percent of the Planet with Renewables," *Scientific American*, October 26, 2009; Fiona Harvey, "Renewable Energy Can Power the World, Says Landmark IPCC Study," *Guardian*, May 9, 2011.

24. Justin McCurry, "Japan Doubles Fukushima Radiation Leak Estimate," *Guardian*, June 7, 2011.

25. Dahr Jamail, "Fukushima: It's Much Worse Than You Think," *Al Jazeera* English, June 16, 2011.

26. David Schwartzman, "Solar Communism," *Science and Society* 60, no. 3 (Fall 1996): 307–31.

27. Trainer, *Renewable Energy*.

28. Elizabeth Kolbert, *Field Notes from a Catastrophe: Man, Nature, and Climate Change* (New York: Bloomsbury, 2006); Kim Stanley Robinson, *Red Mars* (New York: Bantam Spectra, 1993).

29. Murray Bookchin, *The Ecology of Freedom* (1982; repr., Oakland, CA: AK Press, 2005), 349.

30. Murray Bookchin, *Post-Scarcity Anarchism* (Oakland, CA: AK Press, 2004), iii, ix; Murray Bookchin, *Toward an Ecological Society* (Montreal: Black Rose, 1980), 67.

31. George Monbiot, *Heat: How to Stop the Planet from Burning* (Cambridge, MA: South End Press, 2009), 170–88; "Solar-Powered Blimp Set to Fly across Channel," *Guardian*, July 8, 2009; "Solar Impulse Completes 24-Hour Flight," *Guardian*, July 8, 2010.

32. "Solar-Powered Boat Türanor Raises Hopes of a Sun-Fuelled Future," *Guardian*, April 1, 2010.

33. Jason Adams, "Non-Western Anarchisms: Rethinking the Global Context" (Johannesburg: Zabalaza Books), 118; Paul Sharkey, *The Federacion Anarquista Uruguaya (FAU): Crisis, Armed Struggle and Dictatorship, 1967–1985* (Berkeley, CA: Kate Sharpley Library, 2009).

34. Noam Chomsky, *Hopes and Prospects* (Chicago: Haymarket Books, 2010), 118.

35. Michael Hardt and Antonio Negri, *Empire* (Cambridge, MA: Harvard University Press, 2000), 413.

36. Noam Chomsky, "Students Should Become Anarchists," June 14, 2011, available at http://www.chomsky.info/interviews/20110614_en.htm.

37. On grain requisition, see Orlando Figes, *A People's Tragedy: The Russian Revolution, 1891–1924* (New York: Penguin, 1996), 775–80. On the repression of anarchists, see Emma Goldman, *My Two Years in Russia* (Saint Petersburg, FL: Red and Black Publishers, 1924), 199–209; Paul Avrich, *The Russian Anarchists* (1967; repr., Oakland, CA: AK Press, 2005), 222–25. On the fate of the soviets, see Figes, *A People's Tragedy*, 684-90. On Kronstadt and the Makhnovshchina, see Paul Avrich, *Kronstadt 1921* (Princeton, NJ: Princeton University Press, 1970); Paul Avrich, *The Russian Anarchists* (New York: W. W. Norton, 1980), 220–21; Alexandre Skirda, *Nestor*

Makhno—Anarchy's Cossack: The Struggle for Free Soviets in the Ukraine, 1917–1921 (Oakland, CA: AK Press, 2003).

38. Subcomandante Insurgente Marcos, *Nuestra Arma es Nuestra Palabra*, ed. Juana Ponce de León (New York: Siete Cuentos Editorial, 2001), 103.

39. Quoted in Hannah Arendt, *Origins of Totalitarianism* (1951; repr., San Diego: Harcourt, 1968), 473.

40. Arundhati Roy and David Barsamian, *The Checkbook and the Cruise Missile* (Cambridge, MA: South End Press, 2004), 156.

41. Derrida, *Specters of Marx*, 106–7.

42. Georg Lukács, *Destruction of Reason* (Torfaen, Wales: Merlin Press, 1980), 850–52.

43. C.L.R. James, *The Black Jacobins* (1938; repr., London: Penguin, 2001), 215.

44. Robert W. Stookey, *South Yemen: A Marxist Republic in Arabia* (Boulder, CO: Westview Press, 1982); Fred Halliday, *Revolution and Foreign Policy: The Case of South Yemen, 1967–1987* (Cambridge: Cambridge University Press, 1990).

45. Glenn Greenwald, "Wikileaks Cables and the Iraq War," Salon, October 23, 2011.

46. Nick Davies, "Afghanistan War Logs: Task Force 373—Special Forces Hunting Top Taliban," *Guardian*, July 25, 2010; Damian Carrington, "WikiLeaks Cables Reveal How US Manipulated Climate Accord," *Guardian*, December 3, 2010; "WikiLeaks Cables Reveal U.S. Efforts to Defend Cluster Bombs around the World," *Democracy Now!* September 19, 2011.

47. Max Horkheimer, *Eclipse of Reason* (1947; repr., London: Continuum, 2004), 108; see also Castoriadis, *The Castoriadis Reader*, 251; Warner Sachs, "Global Ecology and the Shadow of 'Development,'" in *Global Ecology: A New Arena of Political*

Conflict (London: Zed, 1993), 3–21.

48. Andrew Cornell, *Oppose and Propose! Lessons from Movement for a New Society* (Oakland, CA: AK Press, 2011).

49. "India Anti-nuclear Protest Turns Violent," *Al Jazeera English*, April 20, 2011; "Protest against Koodankulam Nuclear Plant in Pictures," *Countercurrents*, September 19, 2011; Nirmala Ganapathy, "Anti-nuclear Protests Gain Strength in India," *Asia News Network*, November 14, 2011.

50. Helen Pidd, "Germany to Shut All Nuclear Reactors," *Guardian,* May 30, 2011.

51. Murray Bookchin, *The Philosophy of Social Ecology: Essays on Dialectical Naturalism* (Montreal: Black Rose, 1990), 132; Murray Bookchin and Janet Biehl, "Advisory Board Resignation Letter," *Democracy and Nature* 3, no. 3 (1997).

52. A.G. Schwarz, Tasos Sagris, and Void Network, eds., *We Are an Image from the Future: The Greek Revolt of December 2008* (Oakland, CA: AK Press, 2010), 334.

53. Adorno, *Minima Moralia*, 60.

54. Hannah Arendt, *The Promise of Politics*, ed. Jerome Kohn (New York: Schocken Books, 2005), 96.

55. Ramor Ryan, *Zapatista Spring* (Oakland, CA: AK Press, 2011), 48, 208–11; Niels Barmeyer, *Developing Zapatista Autonomy* (Albuquerque: University of New Mexico Press, 2009).

56. Aliza Marcus, *Blood and Belief: The PKK and the Kurdish Fight for Independence* (New York: New York University Press, 2007), 222.

57. Ibid., 89–96, 111, 172–74, 301–5.

58. Rabindra Ray, *The Naxalites and Their Ideology* (Delhi: Oxford University Press, 1988), 230.

59. Samir Amin, "2011: An Arab Springtime?" *Monthly Review*, June 2, 2011, available at http://monthlyreview.org/commentary/2011-an-arab-springtime.

60. Ibid.

61. Gilbert Achcar, *The Arabs and the Holocaust*, trans. G. M. Goshgarian (New York: Metropolitan, 2009), 244–45.

62. Ramachandra Guha, *India after Gandhi: The History of the World's Largest Democracy* (New York: HarperCollins, 2007), 108–10.

63. Ibid., 423–27.

64. Samarendra Das and Felix Patel, *Out of This Earth: East India Adivasis and the Aluminum Cartel* (New Delhi: Orient BlackSwan, 2010).

65. Ray, *The Naxalites*; Arundhati Roy, *Broken Republic* (New Delhi: Penguin, 2011).

66. Roy, *Broken Republic*, 121.

67. Jason Burke, "More of World's Poor Live in India Than in All Sub-Saharan Africa, Says Study," *Guardian,* July 26, 2010.

68. Friedrich Engels, *The Origin of the Family, Private Property, and the State* (1891; repr., New York: Pathfinder, 1972), 61–83.

69. Douglas Fry, *Beyond War: The Human Potential for Peace* (Oxford: Oxford University Press, 2007).

70. Albert Einstein, "Why Socialism?" *Monthly Review*, May 1949.

71. Theodor W. Adorno, *Problems of Moral Philosophy*, trans. Rodney Livingstone (1963; repr., Stanford, CA: Stanford University Press, 2001), 150.

72. Pierre Clastres, *Archeology of Violence*, trans. Jeanine Herman (1980; repr., New York: Semiotext[e], 1994); Giorgio

Agamben, *Remnants of Auschwitz: The Witness and the Archive*, trans. Daniel Heller-Roazen (New York: Zone Books, 2002), 63–64.

73. Michel Foucault, *Power/Knowledge: Selected Interviews and Other Writings, 1972–1977*, ed. Colin Gordon (New York: Pantheon Books, 1980), 121.

74. James C. Scott, *The Art of Not Being Governed* (New Haven, CT: Yale University Press, 2009).

75. Harvey, *Enigma of Capital*, 260, 248.

76. Arendt, *Origins of Totalitarianism*; Wilhelm Reich, *Mass Psychology of Fascism* (New York: Farrar, Straus and Giroux, 1970).

77. Andrew Glikson, "The Atmosphere Is Not Waiting for Human Decision," *Countercurrents*, November 30, 2009.

78. Mark Carey, *In the Shadow of Melting Glaciers: Climate Change and Andean Society* (Oxford: Oxford University Press, 2010), 18.

79. Hannah Arendt, *The Human Condition* (Chicago: University of Chicago Press, 1958), 256.

80. Theodor W. Adorno, *Negative Dialectics*, trans. E. B. Ashton (London: Routledge, 1973), 404.

Credits for Anarchist Interventions

Javier Sethness-Castro

Javier is an educator, translator, and rights advocate born in the U.S. Pacific Northwest. Among his less alienating labor experiences he can count his work for a year as a human rights observer with the International Service for Peace in southeastern Mexico. Since his youth, he has been engaged in transnational Palestine solidarity and antisystemic efforts, and over the past decade has at times intervened as a journalist. In recent memory, Javier has been involved in the Los Angeles and East Bay chapters of Food Not Bombs, Occupy Oakland, and the Gay Men's Health Collective at the Berkeley Free Clinic. He recently presented at the Marcuse Society Critical Refusals Conference on a panel titled Erotic Struggle and at the Los Angeles Anarchist Bookfair. Javier's work has appeared in a variety of periodicals, including *Countercurrents*, *Climate and Capitalism*, *Dissident Voice*, *MRZine*, *Perspectives on Anarchist Theory*, and *Truthout*.

Paul Messersmith-Glavin

Paul was a founder of the Youth Greens as well as a member of the Love and Rage Revolutionary Anarchist Federation. He is a board member with the Institute for Anarchist Studies, an editorial collective member for the journal *Perspectives on Anarchist Theory*, and belongs to the Parasol Climate Collective and the Industrial Workers of the World. His essay "Between Social Ecology and Deep Ecology: Gary Snyder's Ecological Philosophy" appears in *The Philosophy of the Beats* (University Press of Kentucky, forthcoming). Paul is an avid bike rider and community acupuncturist.

Institute for Anarchist Studies

The IAS, a nonprofit foundation established in 1996, aims to support the development of anarchism by creating spaces for independent, politically engaged scholarship that explores social domination and reconstructive visions of a free society. All IAS projects strive to encourage public intellectuals and collective self-reflection within revolutionary and/or movement contexts. To this end, the IAS awards grants twice a year to radical writers and translators worldwide, and has funded some ninety projects over the years by authors from numerous countries, including Argentina, Lebanon, Canada, Chile, Ireland, Nigeria, Germany, South Africa, and the United States. It also publishes the online and print journal *Perspectives on Anarchist Theory* as well as the new Lexicon pamphlet series, organizes the Renewing the Anarchist Tradition conference, offers the Mutual Aid Speakers List, and collaborates on this book series, among other projects. The IAS is part of a larger movement seeking to create a nonhierarchical society. It is internally democratic and works in solidarity with people around the globe who share its values. The IAS is completely supported by donations from anarchists and other antiauthoritarians—like you—and/or their projects, with any contributions exclusively funding grants and IAS operating expenses; for more information or to contribute to the work of the IAS, see http://www.anarchiststudies.org/.

AK Press

AK Press is a worker-run collective that publishes and distributes radical books, visual and audio media, and other material. We're small: a dozen people who work long hours for short money, because we believe in what we do. We're anarchists, which is reflected both in the books we provide and the way we organize our business. Decisions at AK Press are made collectively, from what we publish, to what we distribute and how we structure our labor. All the work, from sweeping floors to answering phones, is shared. When the telemarketers call and ask, "who's in charge?" the answer is: everyone. Our goal isn't profit (although we do have to pay the rent). Our goal is supplying radical words and images to as many people as possible. The books and other media we distribute are published by independent presses, not the corporate giants. We make them widely available to help you make positive (or hell, revolutionary) changes in the world. For more information on AK Press, or to place an order, see http://www.akpress.org/.

Justseeds Artists' Cooperative

Justseeds Artists' Cooperative is a decentralized community of twenty-two artists who have banded together to both sell their work, and collaborate with and support each other and social movements. Our Web site is not just a place to shop but also a destination to find out about current events in radical art and culture. We regularly collaborate on exhibitions and group projects as well as produce graphics and culture for social justice movements. We believe in the power of personal expression in concert with collective action to transform society. For more information on Justseeds Artists' Cooperative or to order work, see http://www.justseeds.org/.

Anarchist Intervention Series

Anarchism and Its Aspirations, by Cindy Milstein (2010)

Oppose and Propose! Lessons from the Movement for a New Society, by Andrew Cornell (2011)

Decolonizing Anarchism: An Antiauthoritarian History of India's Liberation Struggle, by Maia Ramnath (2011)

Imperiled Life: Revolution against Climate Catastrophe, by Javier Sethness-Castro (2012)

Anarchists Against the Wall: Direct Action and Solidarity with the Palestinian Popular Struggle, edited by Uri Gordon and Ohal Grietzer (forthcoming)

Support AK Press!

AK Press is one of the world's largest and most productive anarchist publishing houses. We're entirely worker-run and democratically managed. We operate without a corporate structure—no boss, no managers, no bullshit. We publish close to twenty books every year, and distribute thousands of other titles published by other like-minded independent presses from around the globe.

The Friends of AK program is a way that you can directly contribute to the continued existence of AK Press, and ensure that we're able to keep publishing great books just like this one! Friends pay a minimum of $25 per month, for a minimum three month period, into our publishing account. In return, Friends automatically receive (for the duration of their membership), as they appear, one free copy of every new AK Press title. They're also entitled to a 20% discount on everything featured in the AK Press Distribution catalog and on the website, on any and every order. You or your organization can even sponsor an entire book if you should so choose!

There's great stuff in the works—so sign up now to become a Friend of AK Press, and let the presses roll!

Won't you be our friend? Email friendsofak@akpress.org for more info, or visit the Friends of AK Press website: http://www.akpress.org/programs/friendsofak